Get Up
AND
WALK

JEWELS A. STAIGER

Ellechor
PUBLISHING HOUSE

Ellechor Publishing House, LLC
Beaverton, Oregon

Unless otherwise notes, all scriptures are taken from the New King James Version, © 1984 by Thomas Nelson, Inc., Publishers. Used with permission.

Edited by Andrea J.A. Hall & Rachel Schade
Cover design by Caroll Atkins, C.A. Sly Design
Interior design and typeset by Katherine Lloyd, The DESK

Ellechor Publishing House
PO Box 5489, Beaverton, OR 97006

2011 Ellechor Publishing House Paperback Edition
Staiger, Jewels, 1962-
Get Up and Walk!/ Jewels Staiger.

ISBN 978-0-9826242-4-1

Library of Congress Control Number: 2011922890

Printed in the United States of America

www.ellechorpublishing.com

Dedication

Jesus Christ—I dedicate this to You first and foremost. I promised You I would tell my story. Here it is! I would not be here without You, nor would I have been able to write this without You. Jesus, You are my Savior and my Lord and the Great Physician that heals and restores.

Dave—My husband, my pastor, my friend. I love you honey, and would not have been able to do this without your encouragement and support.

Trevor, Abigail and Dylan—My three little blessings. You three give me a reason to get up each morning, and you are the reason I am so tired at night! Thank you for putting up with mommy and giving her space to write her book—'our story.' There have been a lot of days and nights that I had to work on the book, and although it was hard on you, you have been mommy's biggest fans. I love you more than you will ever know, yet Jesus loves you even more! That is amazing to me! You are the biggest blessings of my life!

Mom and Dad—You are the BEST parents in the ENTIRE world! God knew what He was doing when He gave me parents like you! You have been my strength and my biggest supporters throughout the years. Whenever I hear Celine Dion's Song—"Because You Loved Me" it is the two of you that I think of. I love you. Thank you for all that you have done for the trio, and me, Dave and for always supporting me and then us!

Contents

Introduction

In the Old Testament book of Joshua, there is a conversation between Joshua and God. Joshua said, "Oh, oh, oh...Master, God. Why did you insist on bringing this people across the Jordan? To make us victims of the Amorites? To wipe us out? Why didn't we just settle down on the east side of the Jordan? Oh, Master, what can I say after this, after Israel has been run off by its enemies? When the Canaanites and all the others living here get wind of this, they'll gang up on us and make short work of us—and then how will you keep up *your* reputation?" [1]

Haven't we all felt like this before? We chastise God for bringing us to where we are in life. We ask Him why in the world He would bring us this far, only to hurt. Why would He bring us to a great point in life, only to lose a loved one, or a job, or a home? Why in the world would He allow us to have children that we can't provide for the way we want to or should? Why, God? Why do You let us hurt?

God's answer to Joshua, and I believe, His answer to us, is in the very next verse: "God said to Joshua 'Get up! Why are you groveling?'"[2]

WOW! Even in the Old Testament, God was telling Joshua to quit his whining and Get Up and Walk. He basically told him, "Quit your complaining and do what I tell you to do and

---

1   Joshua 7:7-9, *The Message Bible*

2   Joshua 7:10, *The Message Bible*

everything will work out just fine. Stop being such a worrywart!"

Have you been groveling? I'm sure you have; if not now, then in the past. I know I have. There have been times I've screamed at God. Times that I questioned Him and His love for me. However, God has never turned His back on me. He just keeps telling me, "Get Up! Keep going; you can't quit now. I have some great plans for you, but if you are too busy groveling or wallowing in your pain, then you will not be able to see those plans clearly, so *get up*!"

I do not know what you are going through or the reason why you picked up this book. What I do know is that every one of us has a story. Each of us has something that God has brought us through, and without Him we would not have made it to this day. I also know God wants us to share our testimony with others in order to lift one another up and strengthen each other.

In this book, I will be sharing my testimony with you. At the end of each chapter, you will find a "Faith Walk" devotional, where together we can grow in our faith. The Faith Walk will include a scripture, a question or two to get you thinking, and a few words of encouragement or a prayer so that you too can Get Up and Walk, when God calls your name.

FAITH WALK

* *Read Joshua 7*

* *Why was Israel defeated by the men of Ai?*

* *What was the Lord's response to Joshua's complaint?*

We have all questioned God at some point in our lives only to find out that the problems we were facing were because we had "committed a trespass" (Joshua 7:1) like Achan did. Of course, this is not always the case, because Job was righteous throughout his persecution and did not sin. Yet let us pray now and sanctify ourselves like the children of Israel. Let us pray that we would remove sin from our lives and allow the Holy Spirit to speak to us, and that we learn to walk by faith and not by sight.[1]

> *"Before asking God to bless your mess,*
> *maybe you should ask Him to remove your mess,*
> *so that you can be blessed!"*
> ~Jewels

---

1   2 Corinthians 5:7

I SHALL RISE[1]

Rejoice not my enemy, for I shall rise
You can take my body, but I shall rise.
When you make me fall, I shall rise.
The Lord will be my light, and I shall rise,
Woe is me! When you come at night,
You may slay me, but I shall rise.
You may make me sick, but alas I shall rise,
The politicians and rich man may take my bread,
Oh! Man, He is good, for I shall rise.
You have falsely testified against me, but I shall rise,
Hear you what the Lord says, arise content,
The Lord's voice cries unto me now, you will rise.
The Lord has shown me what is good,
and what He requires of me,

To do justly, to love mercy, and to walk humbly before Him,
His love is true and strong, and I shall rise.
Therefore I will look unto the Lord;
I will wait for the God of my salvation
My God will hear me and I will rise.

–R. W. R. 12/02/2009

Dedicated to my son Jamie Rucker 12/04/2009
With all my Love, Dad

---

1   By Randall W. Rucker

Chapter 1

"GROWING STRAIN"

ONE OF THE SEVERAL MEANINGS of the word strain is, "Eloquent language or words. Language that is eloquent, passionate, poetic or otherwise heightened." That is how I choose to view my "growing up years." Most people call them growing pains, but I choose to call them Growing Strains. The words you are about to read are going to show you what led me to where I am today! I view it as "passionate and poetic."

I am child number six of seven. There are only two of us girls, and there are 12 years between us, so I mostly grew up with my brothers that were closest to my age. My oldest brother Randy is 14 years older than me. Most of my childhood was spent knowing him as a married man to my sister-in-law Ronda. I still remember the boxes they would send me for my birthday when I was a little girl. I loved receiving the gifts they would pack inside.

Next in line is my sister Diana. Although she and I never had the chance to be little girls at the same time, we became close the older I got, and she's my best friend to this day. We've shared some truly amazing life experiences together.

After Diana is Marty. He and I would fight like cats and dogs growing up. Whenever he was left in charge when Mom and Dad went out on a date, Marty and I would end up yelling at each other. I would go to my room and slam the door, and he would follow me just to yell at me some more. Later in life when I became ill, our relationship took a turn for the better. I know I can depend on my big brother for just about anything now. I know that if I called him today for help, he would be there for me.

My brother Mark is next. Mark is a conundrum. I looked up to him as a little girl, and I loved him fiercely. He's funny, handsome and smart. He used to come up with the silliest nicknames for me when I was little and would make the grossest concoctions for our younger brother Jamie and I to drink on a dare. Mark is someone I've always tried to rescue. He intimidates me, yet I long to be around him. He makes me angry, but I can't help but constantly forgive.

Following Mark is Danny. Danny has always been the caretaker of the family. I can remember being on the bus together when I was in kindergarten when he was in fifth or sixth grade. Although I obviously knew that the bus was in front of our home and it was our turn to get off, he made sure to get my attention and wave at me to "come along". Danny has been a friend and confidant over the years, and has never stopped watching out for me.

Last but not least is our youngest brother Jamie. Only fifteen months separate us, and when we were teenagers, we were often asked if we were twins. Although Jamie is a blonde and I've always had dark hair, we look a lot alike.

Actually, we all look quite a bit alike. I can't tell you how many times over the years that I would meet someone for the first time, and they would say to me, "You must be a Rucker." With all of the in-laws and nieces and nephews, we are a rather large group.

When I was young, and my dark hair was long and thick, my mom would put *many* barrettes in it to keep it out of my face. Still to this day when I talk to my grade school friends that is what they remember the most—barrettes.

Twelve was an awkward age for me; I still wanted to play with dolls at home, yet started talking about boys with my friends.

I remember one autumn afternoon in particular. The sun was shining and the sky was blue. I can still see where I was standing and the direction I was facing outside my home. I was on the hill in the backyard, near the huge lilac bush and our rope and board swing. I often dreamed about someday being a wife and mommy, pushing a stroller with twins... a boy and a girl. I always loved to play with dolls, and would often talk my brother Jamie into playing "Adoption Agency" with me when we were younger. I had such a great mom that I wanted to do the same things for my children as she did for my brothers, sister, and I when we were growing up.

Around that same time in my life, I had a strong desire to make "The Church" my life. I had hoped that someday I would marry a pastor, and would always be heavily involved in the church. In my young heart, I never put together that I was being called to anything, but that memory always stuck with me. I don't remember ever telling anyone about this; I just always had it in my head and in my heart that those things would someday be a part of my life.

I had thought and prayed long and hard about writing a book, and one day sharing my story with others. I told my sister a long time ago that I felt like God wanted me to do something big! That I was supposed to travel and sing, but I wasn't sure what it was that I was supposed to share. After all, I was not a preacher, and I still had not met my husband or even knew where I would start! I didn't even *like* public speaking! "What in the world is God calling ME to do?" I would often wonder, but then

I heard that Still Small Voice say, "Just wait..."

I didn't know what I was waiting on, but I felt like He was working on something; and when God is working on something in your life, you listen! So far, He has not failed me. Looking back, I realize that God was preparing me for many things. Some of which were not to be very pretty things, but they made me who I am today.

Who am I today? I am someone who loves to speak and sing in order to share the story God has now given me. I am a woman who, as a friend once described, "Has come through the fire, yet does not smell of smoke." I don't say that to brag; I say that to impress upon you that no matter what we go through in life, we don't need to carry our baggage around with us. We can use our past to help others, without stinking! "For the gifts and the calling of God are irrevocable."[1] Or as *The Message Bible* reads, "God's gifts and God's call are under full warranty—never canceled, never rescinded."[2]

WOW! Once God calls you to something, He does not change His mind! He does not "cancel the calling!" When He calls you, He calls you!

What has He called you to do? Are you listening? Does He want you to change the way you parent? Maybe your calling is to teach a Sunday school class, or clean the church. Whatever it is, it is definitely a calling. God needs all of the parts of the Body of Christ, not just a few. I've come to realize that being called is an honor and a privilege, not something scary to be feared.

I used to think that if He called me to do something, it would be the exact opposite of what the desire of my heart was—I was just so sure of it! He would make me do something that I dreaded and

---

1   Romans 11:29, NKJV
2   Romans 11:29, *The Message Bible*

hated doing. The funny thing is, as I've grown in my faith, I have found that God is not that way at all!

When the Bible says, "Delight yourself in the Lord, and He will give you the desires of your heart,"[1] I don't think that means God is going to give us everything we want. I believe it means that He will place desires within our heart that we never saw coming when we are happy in Him. I believe that if we are in tune with the Holy Spirit, He will make our hearts yearn for the things that He yearns for, and we will find ourselves called to do something that we never imagined possible. Then as we pray, grow, and seek Him, He will lead us in the right direction for our calling, which has become our desire. We will even get excited about that thing which we once dreaded.

FAITH WALK

* ***Read 1 Corinthians 12***

* ***What are the different parts of the Body according to this scripture?***

* ***What spiritual gifts are listed?***

If you don't know what your spiritual gift is, I recommend that you ask your pastor to help you find out.

The Apostle Paul essentially tells us in this chapter that we are not all called to do the *same thing*, but we are all called to do *some-*thing! If you have had a burning desire in your heart to participate or head up some sort of ministry, then pray about it. I find that when I'm not really sure of something, and I tell God outright, "You have to show me, because I'm not getting it," He always does.

---

1   Psalm 37:4

If, after taking the time to pray you are still feeling that desire, then talk to your pastor, or those over you within the church body, and tell them about your desire. Do not be offended if they don't "catch the vision" right away. Instead of saying, "This is what God's telling me, so when can I start?"

tell them that you've been praying and still feel the call, and now you would like them to also pray about it *with* you. Don't be afraid to give a period, for example: "Can we both pray about this, and then get together to share what God is telling us?" Then work out a date to get together to talk about the ministry.

Have a plan written out on how you would start and manage the ministry, and be open to what your leader has also been hearing from the Lord.

Remember that he or she was put into their position by the King of Kings, and although they are human and able to make mistakes or *bad calls* at times, we are still to submit to those God has put into authority when it comes to these things.[1] God will bless us for it.

---

1   Titus 3:1

Chapter 2

WHERE IT
ALL BEGAN

MY PARENTS DECIDED TO MARRY after only three days of knowing one another. Yes, you read that right: three days, three dates, and then a marriage proposal and acceptance. My maternal grandfather was the District Superintendent for the Nazarene Church at the time, in Akron, Ohio—Reverend C.D. Taylor. He was very influential within the church. He and my grandmother traveled almost every Sunday to different churches within the district in order to stay connected to the pastors that depended on him for his leadership.

However, my mother and her younger sister did not travel with them. My grandparents believed that they should have a steady church to attend and a youth group to be a part of. Thus, my mother and her sister went to the church led by their older sister and her pastor husband. This church also happened to be where my dad's family attended.

While Dad was home on leave from the Navy, he asked his

parents if he could have a party at the house for Valentine's Day. His parents agreed. One Sunday morning before the party, he saw a beautiful girl at his church that he had never seen before. He wanted to invite her to the party himself, but was too afraid. He was relieved to see that she showed up with some other teenagers anyway! He asked if he could take her home that night, and she agreed! Over the next two days, he asked her out and each time she said yes.

On the third day, third date, my "Future Dad," took my "Future Mom" on a drive. He stopped by an open field under a beautiful tree and asked her to be his wife. Mom immediately said yes, and they drove to my grandparents' house to tell them the great news.

Granny was sewing, as I always remember her doing, and they told her first. Without ever looking up, she said, "I knew that was coming."

Then they went to tell Papaw the news and he immediately said to my mother, "Give that ring back! You don't even know each other!"

Although he was adamantly against the engagement, he soon relented and gave them his blessing. Until his dying day, he and my dad were very close and loved each other very much.

My mom and dad went on to have 7 children, 21 grandchildren and so far 1 great grandchild. They have also been married for 54 years and counting!

While I was growing up, my family was never rich, but my parents always seemed to meet our needs. If they weren't met my parents kept it so well hidden from us kids that we never even knew. We had many laughs, good times and camping trips as we were all growing up. We had our share of heartaches and tears too. However, we always rallied together and pulled through as a family.

Although I stayed active in the church throughout my teens, my vision was blurred as it is so many times in adolescence. As I mentioned earlier, there are seven kids in our family, and I am the second to youngest surrounded by brothers. My sister was already out of the house and married before I became a teenager.

For some reason, I had very low self-esteem. I had it in my head that I was fat, so therefore I believed that any time a boy talked to me or looked my way, it was only in disgust. A friend told me in ninth grade, "I used to think you were stuck up because you never really smiled or talked, but now I know you better and know that's not the case."

In junior high, I was picked on, and assumed it was because I must be a *huge* monstrous-looking *freak*! I had never once thought that it might have been because I came across as stuck up, or "*too good*" to talk. Only the ones that truly knew me knew that was not the case.

I did have many good friends, from all different cliques! I think part of the *problem* and the reason I was sometimes given a hard time, was because I didn't do the things that many other kids did. When there was alcohol, I stayed away. While others smoked, I wouldn't even try. Everyone knew I went to church and that I took my faith seriously.

Granted, I know some of the "picking" and "bullying" came from the fact that I didn't have designer clothes, or maybe not the most up-to-date hairstyle (barrette girl, remember?). Kids can be cruel.

By the time I graduated high school, I not only had more friends than I had ever had in my life, but I also had a better image of myself. The only thing I really wanted that I lacked through high school was a boyfriend. I never dated.

Growing up in the 1980's in the Nazarene Church, I was not

allowed to attend dances, so when my friends were all getting asked out for those, I was staying in the shadows hoping no one would ask me, so that I didn't have to say no. I should not have worried, because no one ever asked.

In my early twenties, I met a man through friends that I thought would be The One! He was a chaplain and pastor, and I thought this was exactly what I had been waiting for. We dated on and off for four years, before I finally got wise, and broke it off for good. During the entire four years, I was never truly happy. I think I cried more during those four years than I ever had in my life up to that point. We all have reasons why we stay with someone and put ourselves through such heartache, and my reasons were many. However, I finally came to realize he was not the one for me, and that I deserved to be properly treated. I deserved to be loved and cherished.

I went on to date a few other young men, but almost gave up and thought that maybe I had misunderstood what God had wanted for me, or that I had messed things up so badly that He would no longer honor that desire and calling that I felt as a young girl. I kept being "fooled" by the Enemy into believing that I could be happy with less than what God had intended.

After several "dating duds" I had made up my mind that there wasn't anyone out there I could trust. Because of the mistakes and the wrong choices I had made in the men I dated, I had convinced myself that I would never find my "Mr. Right," and I became very cynical when it came to men.

Before my Grandpa Rucker died, I remember him telling me, "Don't settle for the first guy that comes along. Be selective." I have wished so many times that I had listened to him.

I don't know why I was so weak like that. I suppose it probably had to do with my lifelong battle with weight. I never felt as if I was enough, or smart enough, or skinny enough. I had a great family that loved me, so it wasn't as if I was missing that love, but I didn't love myself enough.

It took going through the pain of broken relationships throughout my early to mid-twenties for me to finally get to the point that I was happy with ME!

However, no matter what, throughout everything, my family was there for me. My mom and dad just waited out my bad decisions, and then they were there when I needed to break down and cry, to talk or simply be quiet.

Single women, I will tell you this. My Grandpa Rucker was right: "Don't settle for the first guy that comes along." On the other hand, if you are a single guy reading this: Don't settle for the first girl that comes along. Choose wisely, and choose godly.

FAITH WALK

* *Read 1 Corinthians 13*

* *What is true love according to this passage?*

* *Have you settled for less in the past?*

If you are single searching for love, ask God to bring you the mate He has for you, in the time He has for you. Then trust Him to do it and be patient.

If you are married and not receiving true love according to this passage, start praying for it. Start working toward it. The more we show love, the more apt others are to show love back.

God doesn't call us to settle. God calls us to receive His best! If you are in a dating relationship that is ungodly and unhealthy, you need to get out. As hard as it is, and trust me when I say

I understand, you need to break it off and prepare yourself for God's blessings. You know if it's not right. You can feel it in your heart; you just don't want to admit it to yourself. However, you know and God knows.

"Lord, I ask that You touch the lives of those that have just read this chapter. Speak to their hearts, and if they are in a dating relationship that is not of You, help them to walk away. Sometimes, Lord, You give us the strength to Get Up and Walk; other times You give us the strength to Get Up and Walk Away!"

Chapter 3

DIAGNOSIS

THROUGHOUT MY LATE TEENS AND early twenties, I worked at the local airport cleaning the inside of planes. After doing that for some years, I thought it would be fun to be a travel agent, so I dropped out of college and went to travel school. I landed a job working for American Express in corporate travel, and loved my job!

At first, I worked in the "back office" doing all of the filing, mailing tickets, and busy work, but eventually worked my way into a position as an actual corporate travel agent. I loved every minute of the experience, and the other agents I was working with. I learned a lot from them, and enjoyed my time there.

However, during my second or third year there, I started to feel "not right." Even though I loved my job, it was very stressful. There was no way anyone wanted to send someone to the wrong city, or hotel, or give him or her the wrong car! It was a very fast-paced career. In the midst of it all, my personal life was falling apart.

So, due in part to all of the stress, I became so ill that I no longer had an appetite, nor could I keep any food down. I was wasting away to the point that my coworkers, family and neighbors thought that I might be terminally ill or that I had an eating disorder. My family had been so worried, that my dad and brothers contemplated that if things weren't figured out soon they were going to load me up into a car and take me to the Cleveland Clinic.

My doctor at the time wasn't doing enough to try to find out what was going on, so I kept losing weight until I was 'scary-skinny' , and getting thinner all the time. Secretly, I was thrilled to be in a size four for the first time in my adult life, but my family and friends were not so thrilled. They knew something wasn't right.

My sister Diana had come home for Thanksgiving that year, and not realizing how sick I had actually become, saw me for the first time and just yelled, "STOP!" There was no "Hi, Sis, how are you?" or "Sister! I love you!" but one word, and one word only: "STOP!" She thought from the looks of me that I was trying to lose weight, as I had always battled my size, and was losing excessively!

We later had a sincere sister talk and I explained all of the gory details of the symptoms that I had been experiencing. I also told her about all that my doctor was *NOT* doing to help me. For instance, I once called my doctor's office and explained that I was still having the same symptoms. I wanted them to know I was getting worse, and it was starting to scare me!

They called me back and said, "The doctor said to tell you to get Imodium AD or some other sort of over the counter medication, and to get some Pedialyte Popsicles, and that if you're not feeling better in 48 hours, to give us a call back."

I was dumbfounded. It was September of 1998 when I made this call, and I had been complaining of the same problems since April of 1998. I thought of explaining that to the girl on the phone, and sarcastically said, "OK, I'll do that, but if I end up dead…" Then I stopped myself, and just said, "OK, bye."

Even though my sister Diana lived out of state at the time, she would still visit the same doctor whenever she was home. During this particular visit, she made an appointment for me after hearing about what I had been going through. I was willing to go anywhere and try any doctor by this point. I had become so thin, and my heart was working so hard, you could literally see it pumping in my chest as it raised the thin skin of my chest up and down, up and down. To put my hand over my heart would feel like it was literally going to pump right out into my hand at any moment. My heart rate had climbed with every passing day until it was working overtime at about 140 beats per minute, just when I was sitting and doing nothing.

My sister's doctor was a Christian, and I immediately sensed that in him, so I felt at ease. I also felt as though he was finally going to help me after six months of wondering what was wrong.

Imagine my dismay, when after he ran tons of blood tests, he sat in front of me and said, "I still don't know what it is!"

At this point, I broke. The tears flowed, and I just let loose. He stopped what he was doing, pulled his stool in front of me, handed me a tissue and asked me, "What you are thinking right now?"

I sobbed and said, "I'm tired of being sick, I'm tired of people telling me how bad I look, I'm tired of looking in the mirror and seeing how bad I look, I'm tired of my body hurting" –and at this point I choked back a big sob and said– "And my ankle Is HUGE!"

I realize now how funny that must have sounded, but at the time, it was all as serious as a heart attack to me! I could barely walk. I could barely eat, and what I did eat did not stay with me. I hurt from head to toe, and now I had a HUGE ankle!

The doctor had me lift up my pants leg to show him, and in his most educated doctor voice he said, "WOW!"

My ankle had swollen to the size of a large grapefruit! My joints hurt, my body ached and I was depleted of all energy at this point.

That day, he had his office make an appointment for me with a gastroenterologist. He thought that it might all have something to do with either my immune system or my digestive system, and the only way to start figuring that out was to go see a specialist.

It was near Christmastime by now, so when the GI doctor's office called and said they could get me in on February 14, 1999, I about lost it again! I called my new doctor and he actually got on the phone with me. I told him when they scheduled me and said, "I didn't know if you wanted me to wait that long...to tell you the truth, I don't know if I can make it that long."

His response was, "No way. I'll call you back." About an hour later, I got a call back saying that the appointment would be on January 9, 1999 instead.

I will never forget that day, because although the process wasn't pleasant, it was the day I started on the road to recovery. My ministry began that day as well. No, I didn't come out of the hospital and start telling people about Jesus and preaching on the street. Nor did I travel anywhere but to my parents' house, and straight to bed. However, it was on that day that I found out I had Crohn's Disease, started the proper medications, and began to feel "alive" again.

I was finally able, after a year of suffering, to Get Up and Walk, knowing that Jesus had many more plans for me. I knew deep in my heart that there was something more for me to do. I knew that the ministry that I felt called to would soon begin!

As I left the hospital, my dad went to get the car, while my mom and pastor pushed me out to the car in a wheelchair. I was told later that this pastor called to check up on me to see how I was feeling, and spoke to my mom that day, and every day thereafter.

I took a couple of days off work, and ate as if I had just been brought out of a desert and had been starving for an "oasis."

There is a verse in the Bible which states, "Nothing, you see, is impossible with God!"[1] Another version rephrases and reads, "For with God, nothing will be impossible."[2] This verse is often quoted, but do you know where in the Bible it is from? Go ahead, look it up. Because as you read my story, it's very interesting, how exactly it "fits in" with this Bible story, and I never realized it until just recently! Whether it says "is" or "will be"—nothing is impossible with God!

I found it rather ironic that not long before I became ill, I had thought to myself that even though we had gone through some rough times in our personal lives, our family was fortunate to not have any major catastrophes. Then I ended up deathly ill, and my little brother the same!

A month after I was diagnosed with Crohn's Disease, my little brother Jamie had a Grand Mal Seizure and was taken to the hospital only to find out he had a brain tumor. Our family rallied together from all different places and came together for his surgery. My mom, dad and I rushed to Columbus, where he and his family had been visiting with another one of our brothers and family when he had the seizure.

It was one of the scariest days of our lives. We found out that the tumor was the size of a large walnut, and that he would need to have brain surgery. When I first saw him and hugged him, he would not let go. I knew then that he was scared too.

"'But in order that you may know that the Son of Man has authority on earth to forgive sins and remit the penalty,'" He then said to the paralyzed man, "'get up! Pick up your sleeping pad and go to your own house!'"[3]

---

1   Luke 1:37, *The Message*

2   Luke 1:37, NKJV

3   Matthew 9:6

My family filled the waiting room during that surgery, and we prayed and prayed. The next day Jamie was sitting up and eating solid foods.

"Get up and Walk," is what Jesus seemed to say to Jamie that day, and that is exactly what he did. For the next ten years, Jamie had some issues with seizures and headaches, but he was able to walk home from that hospital in such a short time after his surgery that day, that everyone was amazed!

FAITH WALK

* *Read Isaiah 41:10*

* *Have you ever been genuinely afraid for your life or that of a loved one?*

* *What is God telling you through this scripture in Isaiah?*

It's hard not to worry, yet that's one thing God tells us not to do throughout His Word! There are times now, when either I'm talking to my kids, my youth group, or an individual teen, that I ask them, "Do you trust me?" Since I've built a relationship with them I have gained their trust. The answer is usually "yes," and so then I proceed to tell them that what God's Word says is true!

God is asking us the same thing when we worry: "Do you trust Me?" We usually reply with a resounding, "Yes, Lord! Of course I do!" Yet we continue to worry and hold on to those things which we have no control over. Give your worries over to Him today. Give your health, your family, your job (or lack thereof) over to Him, and quit holding on so tightly.

Chapter 4

NEVER SAY NEVER

EVENTUALLY, I MOVED BACK INTO my apartment, and life returned somewhat to normal. I was only 28, and had actually gone to work one day in January of that year and claimed to all who would listen that my New Year's resolution was this: "1999 will be a year of NO MEN! I will not date, or even give anyone the time of day in 1999! I'm going to concentrate on getting better, and I'm going to just enjoy life, my dog, my friends and my family!"

One friend and coworker said to me, "Oh no, Julie, you've done it now!"

I asked her, "What have I *done*?"

She told me, "You will be married before the year is through! I've seen it happen before, and you just did yourself in! The next thing we will all be hearing is that you're getting married!"

I laughed it off, as did my other coworkers, and said to her, "But I'm not even dating anyone! That would be IMPOSSIBLE!"

While I was recovering and getting back into the "swing of things," Pastor Dave started to call me often to ask how I was feeling, and we would end up talking about all sorts of things.

Eventually, I had to mentally kick myself, because I started to see my pastor in a different light. I was attracted to him, and his heart. I even found myself wondering what it would be like having him as the father of my children someday. I saw how much he loved kids, and it touched my heart. I knew I needed to stop these feelings because he was my pastor. Not only that, but Dave was also quite a few years older than me, and it wasn't that long ago that I had tried to fix him up with a friend of mine. Yes! It's true! I had told a single girlfriend of mine, who was more his age, to come and meet him. She came to our church one Sunday, and then asked me to "put something together" so they could see each other outside of church. When I had moved into my apartment around the same time, I invited them both to come to a get-together I was having. At that time, I truly was not the least bit interested in him.

However, one day at church I leaned over to my sister and said to her, "I suddenly find myself wanting to have that man's babies." We both got a case of the giggles.

I really struggled with myself for many reasons. First, Dave was 14½ years older than I was. Second, he was doing his "job" by checking on me and I was just being a silly young girl attracted to her pastor because he was being very kind about it. Thirdly, I also had my "New Year's resolution," to think about. There was no WAY I was going to go back on THAT after announcing it to everyone!

Therefore, I decided to put it out of my mind. At least until the next time Dave and I talked, or he would send me a card, or leave a cute note on the pulpit when I was going to sing a special on Sunday. Then the wheels of my mind would start to turn once again, and my heart would start to soften against my will.

I know you're probably thinking, "A note on the pulpit!" Well, let me explain. As we became closer friends, he would leave a piece of colored paper with either a cartoon or stickers on it. On these papers, he would depict remnants of conversations we had had, or bits of encouragement for me like, "The Lord delights in Julie!" or "Julie sings for Jesus."

The very first time he left one up there for me, I was thrown, and didn't know what to say or do about it! I went back to my seat after my song, and didn't take the note with me. After church, he came carrying it to me and said, "This was for you!" I was not getting it, but later came to realize that they were just between us, and he didn't want anyone else coming up and seeing our "private" correspondence!

During this time, I had been bringing a little girl to church with me named Karen. Karen's mom and step-dad had abused her. You see, I had grown up with Karen's aunt, and until she could come and get her, Karen stayed with her grandparents. She was right down the road from our church so whenever I went to church, I would pick her up on my way and take her with me. As Karen's birthday came up, I told her I would like to do something special with her to celebrate it. I asked her what she wanted to do, and she exclaimed, "Bowling!" I told her we would go bowling, out to eat, and then back to my home for cake and presents before I took her home.

As we discussed plans and got all excited, an idea hit me, and so I asked her, "Would you like Pastor Dave to go bowling and out to eat with us?"

Karen about jumped out of her seat with excitement, exclaimed "Yes!" and told me how much she loved Pastor Dave. So of course, being the kind person I am, and wanting to make her birthday as special as possible, I called Pastor Dave and told him that Karen's birthday was coming up, and she had asked if I could take her bowling. I told him that she wanted to know if Pastor Dave could come too!

Ok, so maybe the conversation between her and me didn't happen EXACTLY like that, but I did not want him to know at this point that it was MY idea! After all, it was true that she wanted him to come with us, right?

We celebrated Karen's birthday, and had such fun together. After bowling, and a game of pool between him and her, we went to eat at a restaurant. As we were leaving, she leaned up and asked us, "Do you guys love each other?" Had I been eating or drinking at the time, I probably would have choked!

Pastor Dave covered us both by saying something to the effect that "All Christians should love each other," and that "We are brothers and sisters in Christ..."

That was not enough to quell the questions though, because she then asked us, "Are you going to get married?"

I think I said something like "Karen, why don't YOU marry Pastor Dave?" and then we just all got silly and changed the subject! What a night!

A week later though, Pastor Dave asked if I had any plans for Valentine's Day, and if I would like to do something with him! I said yes, and we ended up planning dinner at my apartment. It was such a nice night. He gave me gifts, and a card, and we ate dinner then watched a movie together. I started talking with my mom about everything and telling her, "I think I may have feelings for him, but I'm afraid he just thinks of me as a good friend, since he went through such a tough time with me, but sometimes I wonder if he likes me!"

Then Dave wrote me a poem. The poem was about my eyes, called "Julie's Eyes."

On Sundays, several of us would get together after evening services and go get coffee or dessert at a nearby restaurant. One night after we did that, Dave told me he had something he wanted to read to me We got into my car before I went home, and he read the poem to me. The next day at work, my mom met me for lunch and I read the poem to her. I asked her, "So what do you think? Do you think he has feelings for me?" I laugh now at how naive I was, but my mom was just as bad, because she said to me with a sigh, "Gee, I just don't know!"

Dave and I ended up getting very close, and constantly talking about everything under the sun, from past relationships to future plans and dreams, from failures to the hope we have in Jesus! We even got to the point that we finally admitted one night to each other that we both felt the same way, and were both apprehensive about sharing our feelings because of the age difference and the fact that this was a pastor/parishioner relationship! The night that we had this particular talk, we were in our "Sunday night after church restaurant" alone for once and he asked me if he could kiss me. I said yes, and he got up from his side of the table to come over to my side, and we had our first kiss. How *romantic*! I had never had a guy nice enough to actually *ask* if he could kiss me! Keep in mind it was not even now two months since I had proclaimed my singleness for 1999, and here I was falling head over heels in love with my pastor!

We then upgraded from notes on the pulpit to him handing me a note at the beginning of service. One time it said, "Look up at the speaker on the platform!" I would look, and there, not noticeable to others, was a heart sticker towards the bottom of the speaker. Then I would look back to my note and it would say, "Now turn to your right and look at the window." I would look over, and there would be another heart sticker on the church window. He had this sticker placed right beside where he knew my family would be sitting, because like all good Nazarenes, we sat in the same pew every Sunday!

Once when we met for church in the Fellowship Hall on a Wednesday night, my songbook had a note in it. It listed three things I had to do in order.

1. "Look up at the bulletin board in front of you."
When I looked, I saw an index card with the letter "I" on it.

2. "Look over at the chalk board."
I did that, and there, in the middle of a Bible verse written on the board, was taped another index card with the word "Love" on it.

3. "Look up at the piano."
The card said "You."

When I had found all three notes, I looked where Dave was sitting and he was smiling at me. He had been watching me find his notes all over the hall, while everyone else sang.

Dave made falling in love so much fun! On Valentine's Day, which was on a Sunday that year, he had asked me to sit on the middle aisle side of my pew. I had gotten a feeling he was up to something so had invited a few of my co-workers to church that morning. They loved this romance almost as much as I did.

He was giving the children's sermon, and telling the kids not only how much God loved them, but also that there are many different names for God in the Bible. He and the kids named off several, and then he named some more that the children wouldn't have known. When he got to "Rose of Sharon", he calmly picked up a single rose from behind the choir loft, brought it back to me, and kept right on talking to the kids.

No one's attention was on that children's sermon anymore. That Sunday, they all knew that something was officially happening between their pastor and the "Church Babe," as he had started calling me.

On March 23 that year, after constantly seeing each other through February and March, he came over for spaghetti and a movie, and brought me flowers and a card. He asked to read the card to me, so we sat down after dinner while he read another poem he had written inside the card. This was nothing abnormal, as he was always writing things for me and sending cards. However, this night, as the words flowed and rhymed perfectly, and Joe Cocker's "You Are So Beautiful" played softly in the background, Pastor Dave, Dave, MY Dave, ended the poem with "Julie, will you marry me?" We cried and kissed, and of course, I said yes! Then we ran to call our family and friends and share the good news.

Again, remember it was January when I proclaimed "The Year of No Men!"

But the best part of the story is that on June 26, 1999, I walked down the aisle and went from being *me*, to a *We*. Never say something is IMPOSSIBLE, because when God is involved, NOTHING is impossible. In one year's time, I went from being completely heartbroken, as well as broken down physically, mentally and even spiritually at times, to God telling me to "Get Up and Walk," straight down the aisle of a church and into the rest of my life as the wife of my pastor…

FAITH WALK

* ***Read Hebrews 11***

Though we are uncertain of who wrote the book of Hebrews, the writer lists many historically known biblical figures who overcame adversity through faith.

If you know anything at all about those that are listed in this chapter of Hebrews, you know that they were not perfect people by any means. If you don't know the stories surrounding them, I invite you to look them up and read about them.

God did not ask them to "First, be perfect and then I will use you." Instead He wanted them to first love Him. God wants us to first love Him too. Together, He will then work with us to "clean up our act," so to speak. He can do absolutely amazing things with your life, if you will let Him.

Chapter 5

UNKNOWNS

THERE ARE OTHER TIMES IN my life in which God has asked me to walk into the unknown. About six months after Dave and I were married, we answered a call to a church in Michigan. It was tough to move so far from family so soon after getting married, even though we knew the distance could have been worse. Between my illness and then Jamie's, it was hard to pack up and leave my family. However, we would only be three and a half hours away from them, and were feeling excited to live in a house instead of an apartment. Our first year pastoring a church together had its difficulties, but it was a lot of fun experiencing it together. However, a year into being there, we received a call one night from a neighbor of Dave's mom and 'Gramma.' She said that Dave's mom had had a stroke and was in the hospital. We left that night to head home, and went straight to see her.

Mom and Gramma had gone out to eat that day, and Mom had ordered the "Junk Cake". We have always called it that because the cake is so sweet and so huge! It is yummy, but it was the worst thing Mom could have ever eaten as a diabetic. That same day, she not only had a stroke, but also went into a diabetic coma. We stayed by her side for a week, first in the ICU, then in the nursing home until she passed away.

I felt so brokenhearted for Dave—and for myself as well. I wanted more time with her and I wanted the future children we hoped to have to meet her.

Dave had grown up in a broken home. His father was an alcoholic and his parents divorced when he was young. After the divorce, Dave and his mother moved back to Ohio while his brother Don and dad remained in Arizona. He was not close to his father, so I had never met him. His brother Don and nephew Erik both lived in California at the time, so it was only his mother and grandmother that were a constant in his life at this point.

When Dave's mom was alive, he said that he had asked her if she ever asked Jesus into her heart. She told him that she had. Although she never went to church, we hoped that she truly had asked Jesus into her life. We had to believe that we would see her again, someday. When she was in the coma right before passing away, Dave once again whispered to her at her bedside, and told her that if she truly had asked Jesus into her life, that was great; but if not, she could still do it. He wanted that last chance to be able to make sure his mom would be with us again someday in Heaven. Therefore, he whispered in her ear while I prayed in my heart that she could hear him. I prayed that if she had not truly accepted Jesus into her life, she would now.

FAITH WALK

* Read John 3:16

There is really, only one requirement in order to receive eternal life through Jesus Christ. What does this passage of scripture tell us that requirement is?

It is so simple, yet many try to make it so complicated. The thief on the cross next to Jesus did not live a lifetime of going to church, singing in the choir and doing all of the right things. He simply chose at that very moment to believe that Jesus truly was who He said He was: the Son of God.

I'm going to give you the answer to the question above: What is the only requirement to receive eternal life? Believe. That is it—that's all God requires. Yes, once you believe there will be things that God will ask you to change about your life, but they are things that you will desire to change. It will not all happen overnight. You will not suddenly be asked to pack your bags and move to Zimbabwe to live in a grass hut and preach the gospel to Aborigines. (Although, if you truly feel led to do that, then that's great too!)

All God wants is for those He created to love Him back! Think about it: what do we who are parents want most from our children? Their love and respect and time. That's what God wants from us. There is no right or wrong way to do it, no magic prayer, and you do not even have to be in a church full of people to ask Him to be part of your life. Just tell Him that you believe and ask Him in, and there He will be. You will be amazed at the change that will take place in your life if you genuinely ask Jesus to be a part of it.

Although no church will be perfect, because it's full of imperfect people, it's important for us to attend a Bible believing church.

Find one that you're comfortable with, then focus on Him, not the imperfections. Spend time with God, and in doing so, you will be giving Him your love and respect!

Entering the church doors numerous times a week will not make you a Christian, any more than entering the grocery store several times a week turns you into food! It's what you do while in those buildings and what you take home with you from those places that will determine the nourishment you receive each week!

Chapter 6

FORTY IS THE LONELIEST NUMBER

ALTHOUGH OUR FIRST YEAR AND a half of pastoring a church together was fun as I said, it had its difficulties. If you are a pastor's wife reading this, you know that it can be a very lonely job. We had a small church, but we enjoyed very much being a part of the members' lives. We were invited to family gatherings, swimming parties, and dinners. You name it, and they included us in it. It was nice to be included in those things as a newly married couple, and coming from a large family as I did. I missed my family. And to tell you the truth, I missed Dave!

Yes, I lived by myself before we were married, but I had a full time job, and friends and family close by. I would go have dinner with my mom and dad twice a week, and the other nights I would either hang out with friends after work, or spend time with family.

Don't get me wrong, I enjoyed my space and my alone time, but alone time is only fun when you are not constantly alone! In order to enjoy being alone, you have to know what it feels like to be surrounded by people!

Although the people of the church invited us to most of their family activities, that was not an everyday or every week occurrence, so I got lonely!

We found a job for me upon first moving up to Michigan in a small corporate travel agency. I say "we" because Dave was the first to find the ad for the position. I was excited to see that it was a full-time position with benefits and a salary. I would be the only employee handling all of the travel for a company, so it would be very different from when I worked for American Express. Nevertheless, I looked forward to the slower paced atmosphere of an office of one!

Then I went in for my interview, and it was made clear to me right then that I would not be alone, nor would I even be a full-time employee. Once I got there, another newly hired employee (hired the day before I came in) did most of the interview, and the owner just sat there barely saying a word. I felt tricked, but I really wanted a job within my field, so I took it.

At first, it wasn't too bad, although the woman that I was working "under," according to her, was manipulative and never got the truth exactly straight. The situation became worse and worse until one day she wanted me to lie to cover a mistake that she had made, and take the blame myself! In what world is that OK? I refused to do it, so of course she became angry with me.

From there on out, we did not get along very well, and I eventually told her that when the owner came back from her vacation I was going to give my notice. She told me that she felt the owner would back her up in telling me I could just leave "today."

I could have stayed and made us both miserable, but instead I packed up my belongings and left at that moment. I had never been more miserable in a job than I was in that one, and knew that flipping burgers, if need be, would be more enjoyable!

I didn't have to work. Although Dave was not paid a very high salary at this small church, it was just him, our dog, and me. We lived in a parsonage, and the church paid our utilities. I really just wanted something to do! I was used to working every day.

Therefore, after I walked away from a job of my chosen profession, I went and applied at Sears. I hate working retail with a passion, but knew that I would be happier going back to that, than working with someone who wanted to lie her way through life.

There were a couple of teenage girls from our church that also worked at Sears, and so that made it more fun. I got to know them a little better, and that helped as I assisted with the youth group at the church.

The job was only part time, so when I was home, the loneliness still crept upon me. I remember being in our bedroom one day, crying out to God and telling him that I was so lonely! Almost everyone from the church worked during the day and Dave was always over at the office.

When he wasn't at the office, he was out making "calls" on people from the church. He had gone so long being a single man, that he wasn't used to having to spend time at home.

I came to realize during this time that even in a crowd of forty parishioners and friends, a person could still be lonely. God started to open my eyes to realize that even if someone looked happy as they sat in a crowd of forty plus people, they could be a very lonely person. From that time, I have made more of an effort to talk to the ones that are sitting alone, or seem to be the quieter people. Maybe they are just lonely!

I told Dave how I was feeling, and how miserable I was becoming. After that, we both made more of an effort for me to hang out at the church when possible, and for him to come home and spend more time with me when I was there.

It wasn't long after this that Dave saw another ad in the paper. This time it was for a Lutheran church in the area that was looking for a part-time secretary. Although they were hiring through a local temp-agency, I went and applied with the agency, had an interview with the pastor and another board member, and was hired right away. It was such a great answer to prayer. Gloria Dei Lutheran Church in Tecumseh, Michigan, became such a great thing for me. They treated me as their own, and loved me like a daughter. Throughout my time there, I was taken to lunch, loved on and prayed for, and anonymously given an appointment to have tires put on my car, an expense that Dave and I could not afford. Someone saw that it needed done, and made it happen! It was not just a job for me, but also a ministry and an opportunity to be ministered to. True godly love was shown to me, and it gave me friends outside of our church, which every pastor's wife needs.

Through our ministry, Dave and I have both come to understand that while it is important for a pastor to be in the office, and to be available, it's also important for him to spend time with his family. It was at this point that we also realized that we needed to start thinking about having a family!

FAITH WALK

Hebrews 13:1-6 (*The Message*) says the following:

> *Stay on good terms with each other, held together by love. Be ready with a meal or a bed when it is needed. Why, some have extended hospitality to angels without ever knowing it! Regard prisoners as if you were in prison with them. Look on victims of abuse as if what*

happened to them had happened to you. Honor marriage, and guard the sacredness of sexual intimacy between wife and husband. God draws a firm line against casual and illicit sex.

Don't be obsessed with getting more material things. Be relaxed with what you have. Since God assured us, "I'll never let you down, never walk off and leave you," we can boldly quote,
   God is there, ready to help;
   I'm fearless no matter what.
   Who or what can get to me?

* ***Do you ever feel lonely?***

* ***Think about a time you were truly lonely. What did you do to fill up that lonely space?***

* ***What are some positive ways to fill our time when we are feeling lonely?***

You may have heard the story about the child in bed at night, afraid of a storm. She kept yelling across the hall to make sure her parents were still there. Finally her daddy said, "Honey, we are right here, but don't worry, Jesus is with you!" After a while, she yelled across the hall, "Daddy, I know Jesus is with me, but I really want someone with some skin on!"

We all need that, don't we? Are we any less of a good Christian if we need "someone with some skin on?" God Himself said in Genesis 2:18 that it wasn't good for man to be alone, so He created a partner for Adam: someone with some skin on!

Feeling lonely does not make us weak or less of a Christian, it just makes us human. However, when you are feeling lonely, ask God to fill that lonely space in your heart, and do not be bashful about asking Him to send you a friend with some skin on!

Chapter 7

THIRD TIME'S A CHARM?

When we returned home to Michigan after Dave's mother's funeral, we started to talk more about how life was just too short. Since Dave is almost fifteen years older than I am and we had already been faced several times with just how quickly life passes, we started to think that maybe we should look into adopting. We had been trying to get pregnant for most of that past year, and it hadn't happened yet.

Around that same time, there was a woman at the church whose son and girlfriend had a little girl and a baby, and both parents were in and out of jail. We babysat for several couples in the congregation at times. There was one day we babysat the older little girl of this troubled young couple. She was only about three years old, and was a cute little thing. By autumn of 2000, both of the parents were going to go to jail for quite a while, and the grandmother talked to Dave and I about possibly adopting these little girls.

The baby of these two children was with an unrelated family and the three-year-old was with the mother's parents. The older daughter was not in the best of situations.

We went to court as support more than anything for this family. In the midst of the proceedings, when the judge asked the mother if she had a plan for her children, I just wanted to jump up and say, "We'll take them!" Instead, I nudged the grandmother and told her, "We will take them." So she stood up and told the judge. He said that was something we would have to take to a lawyer, and discuss it with him.

That day as we all stood out in the hallway of the courthouse, we saw the couple that had been taking care of the baby. My heart broke for them, as they seemed to really love that baby, and want to be part of her life. As we discussed with our family what we planned to pursue, and prayed about it, we made an appointment with a lawyer that knew the case.

We sat in his office and told him our desire. He informed us that it would be a very difficult process. He said that even if we were able to get the girls, the maternal grandmother was not an easy person to get along with, and would make our lives miserable. We heard him out, and decided to pray about it some more before moving forward. Nevertheless, while we sat there in this lawyer's office, the thought passed through my head as we were listening to him: "Huh, watch me *finally* be pregnant!" The thought almost shook me to the core! I mean, where in the world did that come from? It had not even crossed my mind before that day that I could be pregnant. Still, I didn't go home and take a pregnancy test that day.

In the past, I had taken a test the moment I even had an inkling that I could possibly be pregnant. I could be one day late, and BOOM, I was off to buy a test! However, this time, for some reason, I just didn't. I was in the midst of a Crohn's flare up, and just chalked any "symptoms" I was having up to the flare. A couple of days later I ran into a member from the church and laughingly told her about the "thought" inside the lawyers' office. She took it right away to mean that "Julie's pregnant!"

I had to stop her and say, "Whoa, whoa, whoa, no I'm not, I'm just saying..."

I went home and told Dave about it, and we just laughed it off. We decided in the meantime that we would not pursue the adoption of the two little girls. We felt that the baby was in a good home, and that we would never be able to win custody of the older girl over that of her maternal grandparents. We decided to just make the girls a part of our prayer life, and wait to see who else God had in mind for us.

We moved on and that winter, started to practice the Christmas musical at the church. As the pastor's wife of a small church, that job fell to me.

One Wednesday night, December 13, 2000, while decorating and preparing for our dress rehearsal for the program coming up, the weather decided not to cooperate. A blizzard started up, and because of that, we called off rehearsal. Since Dave and I lived right next to the church, we stayed and continued to decorate. As the night wore on, I told Dave that I was having this feeling that I could possibly be pregnant. Since the weather wasn't too bad yet, and we lived less than a mile from the local Wal-Mart, he suggested I go get a pregnancy test, so I did! I came back to the church and took the test while Dave sat in his office with the box and instructions on how to read the results. When I began to see the result window show something, I looked at Dave and said, "What does that say?"

Instead of answering me, he just asked his own question: "Is it two lines?"

Then I repeated, "What does that box say?"

He repeated, "Is it two lines?"

By then my face gave away the answer, and he read it all too well. I think we both knew the answers to each other's questions before we ever answered them, but finally I told him "Yes," and he said, "Really? Are you sure?"

There were two tests in the box, so Dave immediately handed me the second one and said, "Do it again!"

I laughed and told him he was going to have to give me a minute! It was not something I could just turn around and do again just because he said so!

After a while, and several gulps of water, I took the second test. When we were both sure that it was also a positive test, Dave asked me, "Was that the best test there was? Was it the most expensive one?"

I laughed and told him that I was sure they were all the same, and that a positive was a positive. He mentioned that the instructions in the box said that it was best to take the test in the morning after first waking up. So yes, I returned to Wal-Mart and got the most expensive, best pregnancy test that they carried.

In the meantime, we continued to decorate at the church. A board member who was a friend at the time and the daughter of the woman I ran into at the store a few days before, showed up to help. We couldn't contain it. We told her about the tests, and we jumped up and down and got excited together. We swore her to secrecy!

The next morning I took the third pregnancy test, and yes, it was also positive! That day, I just happened to have a doctor's appointment because I had been getting so many sinus infections. While I was at the office, I told the nurse, "I think I might be pregnant." Therefore, when the doctor walked in she asked me about it, and asked if I had taken a home pregnancy test. I told her, "Yes…three of them."

She chuckled and asked if they were positive, and I told her they were. She told me, "That's a pretty good indication then," and gave me the names and numbers of some OB/GYNs in the area. So far, my twelve-year-old dreams were coming true! It took going over some bumpy roads to get there, but I had my pastor husband; now I just needed that set of twins!

FAITH WALK

* **Read Luke 1:36-37**

This scripture is one of the first miracles in the Bible revolving around Jesus. Although Luke, chapter one is mostly about Mary, the mother of Jesus, who else does this scripture tell us about?

Do you remember that I told you to find the scripture in the Bible where it says, "Nothing is impossible with God?" Isn't it ironic that that very phrase would be about God giving a child to a woman in her old age, who thought she would never have a baby? (I was not in my "old age" but you get the gist.) There have been so many stories about couples not able to have children for years, then once they adopt, are able to become pregnant. Although this does not happen for everyone, God is always able to provide a child for the childless through adoption.

I have family members and friends that have adopted children, or were adopted themselves. Dave and I would have been happy adopting a child or children, but for us, God had another plan.

For you, there is a different plan than ours, and for others a different plan altogether. Be open to what God's plan is for *you,* because there is no one else exactly like you in the world.

Chapter 8

MODERN DAY MIRACLES!

AFTER THE DOCTOR GAVE ME her blessing to see an OB/GYN, we called my parents. Dave was on one phone, and I was on the other doing most of the talking. The conversation went something like this:

"Hi, we just wanted to share something with you," I said when they picked up.

"OK, what's going on?" they asked in response.

"Well, we decided not to adopt those two little girls."

"Why's that?" they questioned.

I explained the reasons, and then continued by telling them, "But we are now getting a different baby."

"Really? Is the mother someone you know?"

"Yes."

Now, my mom was intrigued and took over most of the conversation. Dave and Dad were just innocent bystanders.

"Don't they want their baby?" Mom probed.

"Yes, they want it," I responded.

"I'm not sure I understand. Is it someone from your church?"

"Yes, it is."

"Well, why are they giving up their baby?"

"They aren't."

"What? I'm lost!" Mother exclaimed with exasperation. It's usually my mom that's the first to understand me, but this time it was my dad.

"Are you pregnant?" Dad asked.

"YES!" Dave and I shouted together.

"Oh, Julie, what are you going to do?" Mother questioned.

"I'm going to have a baby!" I exclaimed.

Admittedly, Mom was worried about my health. She knew that ever since I was diagnosed, I had constant flare-ups with the Crohn's. She had seen me waste away to nothing, and then go through a lot with doctors. She was there when I would break down in tears because my health was becoming so unbearable. She watched as my hands would furiously shake at the worst of my illness so that I couldn't even hold a drink. She saw me barely able to walk because my legs and feet were hurting so badly. And it was my mom who came and finished putting up my Christmas tree for me the year that I was so sick. I'm sure she was wondering how I would handle not only the pregnancy, but also taking care of a baby, and myself. So, to clear things up, her question wasn't alluding to abortion or anything like that. Her question was more of an "Oh my! I'm worried about how your body will handle all of this!" It had barely been two years since my diagnosis.

However, as the next several weeks went on, she, along with everyone else, started to get excited about the pregnancy. She even came up in January to help start getting our house in order and ready for a baby, and just to see *her* pregnant baby.

I started to become so sick with "morning sickness" and a Crohn's Disease flare up that lasted morning, noon and night, that I was extremely grateful for not only the help, but also to have my mommy. I had always heard that most women with Crohn's Disease would go into remission during a pregnancy. In my case, that was just not so. It only seemed to get worse. I lost twenty pounds within the first couple of months, instead of gaining any weight.

While Mom was with us that January of 2001, she, Dave and I sat in the living room after a rough day of working around the house with my being ill. Mom and I wanted to go grab sandwiches at the sub shop instead of cooking that night. We were just waiting until my stomach settled a little first before we left. I sipped some tea, and they were very patient with me. Finally I felt like going with her to get some sandwiches.

Just that evening, we were discouraged to see that it had decided to snow again. We went out into the cold and snow to leave in Mom's car. Dave followed us outside with a bag of trash. As we were getting into the car and I started to buckle in, I felt a wave of nausea. I told Mom to hold on, and opened my door to lean out and be sick. The only thing I really remember is my mom yelling "HEY," or so I thought at the time, and then I woke up confused.

I lay there on the ground, my body convulsing violently, and I had absolutely no control over it. I saw the car, and my mom looking at me as though she was terrified for me. I remember wondering if I had just been hit by a car. My mom looked so scared that it was the only thing I could figure had happened.

Just then, Dave came running around the car and came to help me up. I asked them what happened, and Mom told Dave and me that I just passed out, seemingly in slow motion, and then started to have what looked like a seizure.

I asked Mom a bit later why she yelled at me, and she didn't know at first what I was talking about. I told her that as I was getting sick, I remembered hearing her yell, "HEY!"

She chuckled just slightly and said, "Honey, I wasn't yelling at you. I was yelling 'DAVE!' because I saw you going, and I was scared and knew I would need his help!"

After calming my nerves back down, I felt fine. I stayed at the house while Mom went to get food, because at this point I was extremely hungry! We called my dad and told him what happened, and he thought they should take me to the emergency room. I, however, didn't feel sick anymore, nor did I feel "odd" in any way, or worried. We promised him that if I started to feel even slightly ill, we would go into the emergency room; otherwise I was just going to get some rest.

The next day, I called my OB/GYN, Dr. Byrnes, and explained to his nurse practitioner what had happened. She explained to me that sometimes during a pregnancy some women have been known to have a "Petite-Mal" seizure, due to blood levels dropping too low too fast. Since I was out in the cold, and got sick all at the same time, it was probably just a case of my body's levels dropping too low too quickly. She said that as long as I wasn't having any cramping or other problems, that it was really nothing to worry about. Of course she told me if anything like that happened again, or if I started to feel cramping or ill other than the nausea, that I should call them back or go to the ER. I never had another problem outside of the "morning sickness" and regular Crohn's "issues" again, so life went on!

During this time, I started to think more of that vision I had when I was twelve years old about having twins. In light of the illness that I was experiencing, I really was hoping that that dream would become a reality, as I could not see myself going through any more pregnancies after this.

Whenever I would go to Dr. Byrnes for pregnancy check-ups, he would listen to the baby's heartbeat. There was one time I distinctly remember him saying, "Boy, he's a swimmer!" I wondered why and was told that it was because the heartbeat was all over the place! I didn't think anything of it at the time. However, there was one office visit in which I asked Dr. Byrnes if there was any chance I could be having twins.

Keep in mind that I'm the sixth child out of seven kids in our family, and was the last one to get married or have any children. No one so far in our family had had twins, or multiples of any kind. My mom told me after all was said and done that she had actually had an aunt and uncle that had been twins, but I had never even met them or heard about them, as they were before my time. I just always had it in my head that someday I would have twins! It was the desire of my heart.

I always wondered what that phrase "desire of my heart" meant. Having twins wasn't a wish really, or something I even dwelled upon. It's just that there was always something inside me that desired that, and it was really out of my conscious control!

When Dave and I asked Dr. Byrnes if there was any chance of twins, he told us, "I'm ninety-nine percent sure there's only one baby. But, there's always that one percent, and we can't really know until the first ultrasound."

We went home a little discouraged, because Dave had started to catch my vision of twins. Also, because I didn't feel that I could physically go through another pregnancy. However, we just wanted a healthy baby, and we would be happy.

One afternoon, though, when I was in the bedroom by myself

and just couldn't get it out of my mind, I prayed this prayer: "Lord, I know with all of my heart that even if there is only one baby, You could put another one in if You wanted to! I know You could turn the one into two!" At the "Amen", I walked out into the living room, and without telling Dave what I had just prayed, I asked him to help me pick out some extra names "just in case" we had twins.

He sat me down and kindly said, "Honey, you heard the doctor; we aren't going to have twins."

I told him I knew what the doctor had said, but just wanted him to humor me, and pick out an extra boy name and an extra girl name just in case! So we did. I never once mentioned my prayer to him or to anyone else. I felt that it was just something private between God and me, and should not be spoken of. I think it was truly the first prayer I ever prayed that I totally believed with all of my heart God could and just might answer!

On March 23rd, 2001, we went to have our first ultrasound. On the way through the door, Dave and I walked hand in hand and talked about how it was OK that it was just one baby, and that we just wanted to know that it was healthy and were excited to find out the sex.

It seemed that overnight, I had started to gain my baby weight finally, and so when I went in to prepare for the ultrasound, I actually had a belly to look at!

Dr. Byrnes came in and gooped up his wand, and then touched it to my rounded belly. The next words out of his mouth were such a shock that I could barely breathe. He said, "Well, you guys, there they both are!"

"Both?" Dave and I asked in unison, and we looked over at the screen. Sure enough, there was not one, but two little bodies lying on top of each other! I looked at Dave and began to slap him on the chest and say, "I told you, I told you!" Then I looked at Dr. Byrnes and said the same thing!

Just when I thought Dave looked like he needed to sit down, the doctor asked him to poke his head out the door and get a nurse, because he needed more paper for the machine to take another picture.

I just kept repeating to anyone who would listen, "I told you! I told you! I asked God to give me twins and He did it!"

While Dave was busy poking his head out the door, I took my eyes away from the computer screen for just a moment. I was laughing so hard that I couldn't have seen anything too clearly anyway. Remember how I told you in the beginning of this book to read the circumstances around that Scripture? It was Luke 1:37 that said "Nothing is impossible with God!", but I said to read the story around that verse, because it had even more to do with the rest of my story.

You see, this verse was spoken by Elizabeth, when she found herself to be pregnant in her old age, and she laughed! No, I wasn't very old when I was pregnant; I wasn't quite thirty when I found out I was pregnant. But just like Elizabeth, I laughed when I found that God had answered my prayer and the desire of my heart of over twenty years to have twins! I had asked God to perform a miracle! I asked for the impossible, and He answered with a resounding, "YES!"

So I laughed. I laughed out of the joy of my heart for this answered prayer, just as I'm sure Elizabeth laughed when she found out she was pregnant. She wasn't laughing because it was silly. She wasn't laughing because she thought it was a joke. She laughed because she was filled to the brim with joy, and there was no other way to let it out!

Well, while I laughed and Dave poked his head out of the

door, the doctor looked around inside my belly with his little goopy wand!

All of a sudden though, he looked at me ever so seriously and asked me, "Did you see that?"

I'll tell you, the way that he looked at me so seriously wiped the giggles right out of me. I thought for sure either something was wrong, or maybe one of the babies had moved, and he was just hoping I had seen it.

I looked back at him and then the screen and said with trepidation, "No, what was it?"

He looked at me, and with the color drained from his face he said, "I think I just found number three!"

There was about a half-beat pause, and I said, "No way!" as I smacked Dr. Byrnes on the arm!

He replied, "Yes, way! I'm sure of it!"

By the time poor Dave walked back to us, the doctor and I were BOTH laughing. He told Dave, "Dad, you're having triplets!"

Dave's response was, "Yeah, right!"

He hadn't yet even grasped the "twin thing," so when he walked into us laughing and being told he was having triplets, he thought we were pulling his leg!

Once I got it through his head that it was no joke, and the doctor showed us both the proof of another little body behind the other two, Dave joined in with the laughter, and asked, "Is that it? There's no more is there?"

Pretty soon, hearing the commotion and laughter from inside our exam room, the nurses came in asking if they could see and be a part of this day. It was the first time their office had ever had a set of triplets!

For four days, Dave and I kept looking at each other saying "Three?!" And the laughter would begin again!

Dave and I are constantly asked whenever we tell this part of our story, if we had gone through any sort of fertility treatments. Let me say that all children are a gift from God. However, we did not go through any fertility treatments or take any sort of medications to help us become pregnant.

Between my illness and his age, we had decided before we got married that if we weren't able to have children soon after we decided to, that we would just adopt, and be happy with whatever child God gave us.

I'm amazed that God loved me enough to let me become pregnant with triplets, and not only give me the desire of my heart, but also outright bless us with a miracle. There is no other way around it, and no science to say otherwise.

I believe that He had already given us twins, but when I prayed in faith and believed that He could work a miracle, He decided to give us a third child.

I see so many reasons as every year passes why He gave us three babies. You will begin to see some of those reasons in the next chapters.

FAITH WALK

* **Read Acts 9**

Saul was a terrorist. The Bible tells us that men, women and children were all subjects of prey to Saul. He was no respecter of persons. If you were a Christian, he wanted you dead. He killed and jailed Christians whenever and wherever he could. Saul the terrorist is a historic fact. How are Christians viewed today within your social circle?

* **In this passage, what does God do with Saul?**

* *What miraculous change took place in Saul's life?*

God later changed Saul's name to Paul. After his conversion, the Christians did not accept him at first. When everyone realized that his conversion was for real, he was no longer accepted by his Jewish contemporaries and was embraced by the disciples, who then helped him to flee those who now wanted to kill him for converting.

You see prior to his conversion, Saul was not just a hater of Christians, but also a very high official in the Sanhedrin. This meant that Saul was part of a well-educated, highly powerful, greatly feared group of individuals in Rome.

What does all this have to do with a chapter about my pregnancy and having triplets? With God, ALL things are possible. ALL things! If God can turn a mass-murderer into one of the most influential preachers of all time, He can help you find a way to pay your bills and still feed your family. He can lead you to that love you have been searching for and haven't found. He can give you that baby you have dreamed of, the job you are in need of, and bring you through the illness that has taken so much from you already. Trust Him.

Chapter 9

WATER INTO WINE

NOT LONG AFTER WE GOT home from the ultrasound, we had another fun conversation with my parents. Again, with Dave and I each on the phones, we called home and asked Mom and Dad to each get on a phone. The conversation went something like this.

"Hi, Mom and Dad! Well, we went to have our first ultrasound today. Unfortunately, they couldn't tell us the sex."

"That's too bad," Mom responded, " but as long as the baby's healthy….."   "Yeah, well, it was just too hard to tell," I said, then smiled to myself as I added, "since they were on top of each other."

"What?" Mom and Dad said in unison. "What was on top of each other?"

"The babies," I said. "They couldn't tell the sex because they were on top of each other."

"Twins?" Dad asked.

"Oh, no." I answered.

"Huh?" Mom was bewildered.

"We're not having twins," I said.

"But…you said…" Mom was really confused now.

"Julie, what are you saying?" Dad probed.

"We're having triplets!" Dave and I chorused together.

Silence.

"Oh, my, Julie!" Mom exclaimed. "What are you going to do?"

"I'm going to have three babies!" I answered. "They aren't puppies! We can't just give some away!"

Then we all laughed! For days, we laughed! We had similar conversations with other family members and friends, and it never got old! One of the best was with my sister Diana. When we got to the part after she asked if it was twins, and we said "No," she laughed, and very quietly—as if she was scared to even say it, but yet, excited to say it all at once—she asked, "Triplets?"

When we said yes, the three of us were just about in tears! It was the best moment! Calling our family and then friends to tell them was just so special!

Dr. Byrnes immediately referred us to see a high risk specialist in a city about forty-five minutes away, over the border and into Ohio. He assured me that it was only because we were having triplets, and that it didn't have anything to do with the fact that I had Crohn's or because anything was wrong. He explained that it was because he didn't feel comfortable caring for a woman with triplets, and that to be safe, it would be best to go to this specialist. We had such faith in Dr. Byrnes that we did as he said, and made our appointment with the high risk doctor right away.

We made the appointment for the following week, and traveled to Ohio to see this doctor located in the hospital where we would eventually deliver our babies.

It was at this ultrasound that we found out we were expecting two boys and a girl. First she found the two boys. Dave and I were both hoping for a girl in the mix as we waited to find out what the third was. The technician continued to look then said, "Well there's your rose between two thorns! There's your little girl. What a perfect little family!"

As I was lying there having my second ultrasound, the technician called the doctor into the room. I knew after twenty-nine years of life and Crohn's Disease when a technician had seen something wrong. I also knew she wasn't allowed to tell me what she saw. My heart dropped I couldn't take it, so while we waited for the specialist to come into the room, I said to her, "I know you're not supposed to tell me anything, but I need to know what it is. I know that there's a problem. I won't hold you to anything, but you *have* to tell me."

After just a moment of thought, she said to us, "Your baby girl has a two-vessel cord."

We asked her what that meant, and she told us that we would have to wait for any further explanation from the doctor. I knew she had already gone further than she was supposed to and out of her comfort zone, so we didn't push. Dave and I just looked at each other and held hands while I lay there and waited for the doctor to come in.

Pretty soon, this man that I had never met in my life before this moment, came bouncing into the room. He began to look at the screen, move the wand around my belly and point things out to the technician while whispering and nodding his agreement.

My heart cried out to God in that moment and pleaded with Him to make things OK.

The doctor left without a word, leaving the technician to get me cleaned up. After the technician helped me sit up, she said the doctor would return in a moment.

When he came back in, he explained to us that our little girl did indeed have a two-vessel umbilical cord, and that what that meant was that she would be getting less oxygen and less food than the boys. In a single birth, it's not such a big deal, but with multiples it gets a little trickier. He went on to tell us that at the very least she would be very small and have growth problems. We needed to prepare ourselves for the fact that IF indeed she did live, she would probably have a deformity or learning disability. However, he said, "You need to prepare yourselves for the fact that she very well may not make it. You will most likely have to come to the decision to either 'let her go' in order to let the boys go as full-term as they can, or to risk the boys by taking them early to save her!"

Again, there was silence in the room, as Dave and I took it in and felt our happiness fly right out the window.

Nevertheless, this awful man in a white coat didn't miss a beat, and asked us, "Why are you looking so sad? Trying to decide what color to paint the nursery?"

I was dumbfounded! I didn't know how to reply to this man. I told him, "You just told us that our baby girl may not make it, and that we are most likely going to have some hard decisions to make. It does not make a happy mother-to-be."

Then he chuckled and told us to not worry about it until the time came.

On the drive home that day, Dave and I were both worried and scared. We decided that we would call everyone we knew and ask them to pray! We would call churches, both our denomination and not. We would call the 700 Club prayer line and any other prayer line we could think of! We would storm the gates of Heaven for our babies! We were convinced that God had given us three babies for a reason, and that it was all in His hands, but we just didn't want to let go of this baby girl that we already loved!

That night, after making our phone calls, we prayed together.

It had become our nightly tradition for Dave and me to both lay our hands on my belly and pray specifically for the babies that we would name Trevor, Abigail and Dylan. We didn't break tradition this night either, and we stepped the prayers up by pleading with God for the lives of our babies.

After our time of prayer and tears, Dave went to the living room to do his individual devotions, and I stayed in the bedroom to do mine. Before I opened to my scheduled Bible reading for the night, I pleaded with Jesus one more time. I said to my Heavenly Father: "Lord, I know that if You can make the lame to walk, the blind to see, raise people from the dead and turn water into wine, that You can take care of my baby girl and my boys, and let them be born healthy and whole!"

I spent some time just *being* with the Lord, and then I opened my Bible to John chapter 2, where I was scheduled to read for that night. I looked down at the page, and couldn't believe my eyes! The chapter was entitled "*Jesus Turns Water into Wine.*" Was He telling me everything would be OK? I wasn't sure, but I did find comfort in the fact that those were the words I had just prayed, then without realizing it, I was on that very story in my Bible reading!

The next morning I headed to my job as a part-time secretary. Before leaving the house, I looked for some music to listen to that would be uplifting and maybe help me to be more joyful that day, as I was back into my slump by morning. I pulled open a random drawer in my search for something new, and found a Kathy Tracolli tape that I never remembered hearing before. I was running late, so without really looking at it, I put it in my purse, kissed Dave and ran to the car. About fifteen minutes into my thirty minute drive, I heard these words: "Lord, I need a miracle; Lord, I need You! You turned the water into wine… "

I could barely see the road through the tears in my eyes. This was before I had a cell phone, so I had to wait until I got to work in order to call Dave.

I had him a bit worried, I think, as I was in tears as he answered the phone. I tried to tell him what was going on, and explain my prayer the night before, the Bible reading, and then the song. Finally, I got everything out and put the phone up to the tape player in the office so he could hear. I ended by telling him, "Everything's going to be fine! She's going to be fine, and the boys will be fine, and we don't have to worry! I know that everything will be alright. I have such a peace at this moment!"

FAITH WALK

* *Read John 2*

Jesus was not at this wedding just to perform miracles, or even to preach. He was there because He enjoyed the things other human beings enjoyed, and took part in festivities!

* *Have you ever been to a wedding or party where something went wrong and caused embarrassment or shame to the ones throwing the party? How did those in charge handle the problem?*

* *Has God spoken to you before through His Word (the Bible) or through another person?*

God spoke to me the night I read John chapter two. I had not only mentioned Him turning water into wine in my prayer, but twice more the same topic came through His Word and through music.

* *What are some other ways God uses to speak to us?*

Chapter 10

PEACE LIKE A RIVER

As MUCH PEACE AS I felt, there were a few times when that peace was tested. Remember, at this point, everyone knew what the specialist had told us, and knew of the worries we had only the day before. They didn't understand the peace we were now feeling, because they weren't as close to the situation.

Consequently, our faith was tested thoroughly. Satan would use things that others would say to us to try to steal our peace! I was asked, "Are you sure they aren't attached to each other? The babies, I mean?"

Then there was this one: "You know, I've heard of instances where a woman was having twins, and even though one died, the other still lived. The tissue is just reabsorbed by the mother and other baby, so don't worry. Even if one dies, the other two can be OK."

Then there was the church we were pastoring. Even though they loved us and were good people, they kept putting off having a shower for us. A friend of mine finally asked someone, "Are you guys ever going to have a shower for Dave and Julie?" She told me later that her answer had been this: "Well, we decided to wait until after the babies were born, to make sure that all three make it."

My friend went ahead and threw a shower for us at her house, and invited everyone from church...BEFORE I gave birth!

Since some of the comments that were making me fall back into doubt and fear came from some family members, I finally asked my dad to speak to everyone as the "Head of the Family." I asked him to make it clear to them that I was already having a hard enough time, and did not need this kind of "encouragement." He did so, and everything calmed down. We ended up being thrown five different showers in all, before the babies were born!

FAITH WALK

* *Read Hebrews 6:18*

* *What two things has God given us that are unchangeable according to this verse?*

* *Have you ever felt God's peace and presence only to have someone snatch that away through careless words or actions?*

* *The next time God gives you a promise and someone or something tries to disrupt your peace, go back to Hebrews 6:18, because God cannot and does not lie!*

Chapter 11

GETTING PREPARED

FOR THE DURATION OF THE pregnancy, my original OB/GYN Dr. Byrnes saw me on the weeks that the specialist did not. He talked with the specialist about the way he spoke to us at that first visit. Dr. Byrnes added that he was not happy with the way things were handled, and after us, would not be sending anyone else his way.

By the time it was getting close enough to give birth, we asked my regular OB if he would go ahead and do the delivery. He agreed, and we looked forward to delivering three healthy babies.

As the date drew closer, our local paper came to do a story on us, and we made the front page that Mother's Day. We relished every moment of the pregnancy. Even though I still was having morning, noon and night sickness, I enjoyed carrying my babies and the attention that came with carrying triplets!

On April 28th, the day before my 30th birthday, my family planned a baby shower for us back home. I had still been having so many problems with dehydration, being sick to my stomach and even sinus infections, that my regular OB didn't think I should travel home. I was brokenhearted, but in the end, after much prayer and against his advice, I went ahead anyway. We figured there were doctors everywhere. Even in Akron.

We had a great time at the shower. Then the next day for my birthday we went to my favorite restaurant and returned to my parents' home, only to leave shortly after to attend another shower given by my sister-in-law at the church I grew up in. It was such a lovely weekend and everything went just fine.

We returned to Michigan and my friend who had thrown our baby shower with our church offered to come and paint the nursery in the parsonage. Toni was a bit of a hypochondriac by her own admission, so she was very worried about me smelling any fumes. Therefore, I had to sit in the living room while she painted the nursery with an air purifier right next to her. At one point, she went downstairs to the basement to get some supplies, and when she came back up, seemed very concerned. She said, "Julie, there's a black spot on the ceiling down there that just does not look right. Did you know that?"

I told her it was just mildew from a toilet that used to leak before we moved in, and that I didn't think it was anything to worry about.

She wasn't convinced and called to ask her mom to stop by. Her mom went down to check it out, and said the same thing. She didn't think it was just mildew and thought that we should get it checked out. She came upstairs and told me: "It's fuzzy!" She said if it was black mold, it could be harmful to us and the babies!

Dave and I weren't about to take a chance with these little gifts that we had been given, so we called the Health Department to find out how to get a test done. They referred us to a state-approved environmentalist, and he instructed us on how to send two different samples to him to be tested. We sent the samples and didn't think much more about it.

Throughout my most recent appointments with the doctors, we found that all three babies were in a breech position, and were told that no matter what, I would have to have a C-section. The Cesarean was scheduled for July 24th, 2001, but I felt that I would never make it that long.

One Sunday morning, on July 8th, I had slept so poorly the night before, that when it came time to get ready for church Dave insisted that I stay home. I had been spending more and more time in bed. Even though the doctors had never put me on bed-rest, I basically just put myself there.

It started to get so hard to walk and move around comfortably that we set a window air-conditioner up with a fan blowing right at me, along with a TV and rocking chair in our bedroom. I was more comfortable in that room during that time than any other room before or since. I can still feel the cool air blowing on me, and the comfort that it brought.

However, that particular morning as I lay in that same comfortable, cool room and tried to rest, I became restless. All night long I kept having pain in my lower abdomen. Trevor was known to move a lot in that area; however, this night it felt like he was doing flip flops!

I went along with Dave's plan, and stayed in bed and tried to get some rest. He promised that after church we would go to Ponderosa, since I had been craving it for a while. After tossing and turning, I finally felt like I might be able to sleep, and my body started to relax. Just then, my water broke, and I knew two things: I was having babies today, and I was not having any Ponderosa!

I called over to the church and asked our friend Randy, who answered the phone, to tell Dave to come home right then! He stammered and paused, so I said, "Randy, my water just broke!"

Randy quickly stammered some more and said, "Oh, oh ok, um ok!"

It wasn't until later that I found out Dave was right in the middle of his sermon when I called, so when Randy poked his head into the sanctuary to tell him "Julie's water broke," there was a collective gasp throughout the small church. As we drove off for the hospital, everyone from the church stood outside and waved to us as we left, cheering us on! I looked at Dave and said, "Ya'll come back now, ya hear?"

It reminded me of the scene on the old TV show, "The Beverly Hillbillies", when they all would stand out on the porch waving at the end of the show.

FAITH WALK

* *Read John 20:29-31*

* *Who does Jesus say will have even greater blessings in this passage?*

* *Is it easier for you to believe if you see, feel and touch?*

* *If you don't believe in Jesus, what would it take to make you believe?*

It takes more strength to believe in the unseen, than to believe in that which is seen. Any seeing person believes that the sky is blue; that's easy on a clear day. It takes faith to believe that once the clouds pass and the storm is over, the blue sky will inevitably appear once again.

Chapter 12

FROM B-DAY TO D-DAY

WHEN WE GOT TO THE local hospital, we were informed that our regular OB was on vacation and would not be able to deliver the babies. Although we were disappointed, we were just ready to do whatever needed to be done to finally meet our babies.

After being monitored for a bit, they loaded me into an ambulance to transport me to the hospital in Ohio to the specialist. Happily, when we arrived there, we were informed that he was also on vacation, and would not be able to deliver the babies either. I met his partner, who was like a kindly grandfather.

Everything seemed to go so fast, but I do remember seeing my babies being born, and my breath catching in my chest. They literally took my breath away!

We were soon told that all three had APGARS of 9 and were perfectly fine. They were all weighed: Trevor was three pounds and twelve ounces, Dylan was three pounds and two ounces, and Abbey was a whopping four pounds and five ounces! My little girl, who we were told would probably not live, but if she did, would be the smallest of the three, was actually the biggest of my babies!

Earlier in the morning, before leaving the house, I called my mom and dad to let them know we were having the babies. They got a hold of my sister, and by the time I was being wheeled out of surgery behind my babies, they were sitting there waiting. They had already gotten to see my babies being taken to the N.I.C.U. (Neo-natal Intensive Care Unit).

Even though I remember everything leading up to the birth and then the birth itself, the rest of that day is sort of a blur to me. I know that right after I was taken to a room, I couldn't stop shaking. Everyone kept trying to warm me up, only for me to tell them that I wasn't cold, but that my body just wouldn't stop shaking! The nurses told us it was "normal" because of all of the hormones that had just left my body.

I remember then being wheeled in to see my babies, but not being able to actually hold them. My heart broke. That night was very hard for me, being separated from part of myself. The next day, however, when I told the nurse on duty that I had not yet held my own babies, she said, "Well that's just silly; sit right here while I get them for you!"

The next thing I knew I had all three of them in my arms.

The entire time of my pregnancy we were told by all medical personnel that it would take some time before our babies would come home. We were told that it would probably be a case in which one baby came home in a few weeks, and then a few more weeks before the next, and maybe months before all three babies came home.

While I stayed in the hospital for five nights right down the hallway from my precious little ones, Dave stayed in the nearby Ronald McDonald House. I felt myself going through something. Instead of a feeling of elation at being able to go see my babies in the nursery, I felt an extreme sense of loss and sorrow that they weren't with me anymore. I don't believe that I suffered from full blown post- partum depression, but I was going through something that I didn't quite understand.

The day I was released was a hard day for me. Even though I was still close by, it was very hard for me to be even that far from my babies. I checked into our room at the Ronald McDonald house in the evening and waited for Dave to come back from taking care of some things at home in Michigan. I had a good cry, and then lay down to take a nap. I had just started to fall asleep when Dave came back. He looked extremely worried.

He explained to me that the brakes on our new pre-owned van were acting up, and he would need to take it in to get looked at. As if that wasn't enough, he sat me down to tell me that the environmentalist had finally got back to him. He had apologized for taking so long, but was just getting back from a black mold disaster in a Cleveland, Ohio, apartment building where eight children had died.

He asked Dave if we were living in the house, and Dave explained that we weren't yet, but were staying near the babies who were still in the hospital.

The kind man then had told Dave that our tests showed that we had two types of black mold of the worst kind, and we should not under any circumstances take the babies into that house. He said, "As a matter of fact, you and your wife can't even be in that house until it's looked at to see if it's in the joists of the house!" He said if it was in the joists, there was nothing that could be done to clean it, and it would have to be burned. He asked Dave if he and I had developed any sort of allergy symptoms we hadn't had before living there. It was then that it dawned on Dave the reason why I had been having a terrible time with my sinuses like I had never had before! It was the house.

I thought I would break. I lay down on the bed and wept until I couldn't move anymore. We both cried, and then I fell asleep emotionally exhausted.

FAITH WALK

* ***Read Psalm 34:15-20***

* ***Have you ever been broken? Physically? Mentally? Spiritually?***

* ***What does this passage tell us about the relationship between God and the brokenhearted?***

As I finish writing this chapter I am reminded of the pain. It was so deep. But God knew my hurts. He knew all that we had been through up to this point, and He knew what was going to take place in the following months.

As you read and think about the pain in your own lives I pray that God will give you peace. I pray that you will be reminded that God has great things in store for you. Although you cannot see beyond today, God can see ALL of our tomorrows! I pray that you will put your trust in God.

Chapter 13

OUR FIRST
HOME–REALLY?

DURING THE NEXT FEW DAYS, we learned that to get our brakes fixed it would cost us $342.00, and we only had $49.00 to our name. In the weeks that followed, my parents stayed at our "infected" house with the windows open constantly. They began to clean and pack up our belongings. The house was looked at, and it was discovered that the mold was not in the joists. However, the church did not have flood insurance, and it was going to take more money than they had to fix the problem correctly. We were now homeless. Here we had three little beings that were totally depending on us for everything, and we had no home to give them. No roof to put over their heads.

I started to become depressed. I cried every day, and swore everyone to secrecy about our situation. I wouldn't let anyone talk about it whenever we were in the hospital. I suppose I had seen too many movies, but I was terrified that if the hospital personnel would get wind of our situation they wouldn't allow us to take our babies out of the hospital. So, while I sat at the hospital all day holding and feeding my babies, l worried about what we would do!

Once, when my aunt and uncle and the District Superintendent and wife all came to visit in one day, they wanted to go see the babies and have prayer. We went into the N.I.C.U. and joined hands around the babies and prayed. However, when the discussion turned to the mold problem, I made everyone leave the nursery and told them I didn't want the hospital to know about it.

During this time, an envelope addressed to me came in the mail from Canton, Ohio. Not knowing who it could be from, I opened it up, unsure what to expect. Inside was a check for $300.00! Exactly what we needed to make up the cost of getting our brakes fixed. It came from a church that we had absolutely no association with. This was a church that had heard through the grapevine of our circumstances, and wanted to help out. The most amazing part was that they had no idea of the need for brakes. They knew only of the fact that we had these three babies, black mold, and needed another place to live, so they wanted to help out in some way!

Our friend Toni tried to help Dave find us a place to live while I stayed with the babies all day, every day. She even had our need put on a local radio station. We got a call for one apartment. A lady said she had heard our story and would like to help us out. She and her husband had a place attached to their home that they were looking to rent and she offered it to us.

I asked Toni to go with Dave to check the place out and give me a woman's perspective. When they returned to fill me in, they let me know that the molding on the walls was off and needed to be fixed, but other than that, the apartment was fine. The problem was with the people.

While they were looking the place over with the woman, she told them, "My husband doesn't really like kids, but I love babies, and want to help! If you guys are quiet, I'm sure he won't even care."

That took care of that! While visiting, Toni and Dave learned that the couple's living room was right on the other side of the wall of the apartment. I didn't think bringing three newborns into that apartment would have worked. I'm sure we wouldn't have been "quiet enough" for this man, and I for one didn't want to see how that worked out.

The next house that opened up was another parsonage from another church, another denomination. Again, I asked Toni to look at it with Dave and give me her opinion. They drove by and saw that there had been some work done in front of the house. There was some ground dug up. When they asked the previous dwellers about it, they were told that their son had had some respiratory problems, and every October, he would get pneumonia. They came to find out that there had been some water leaking in the basement also, and that's what had been dug up in the front yard.

Ok, how do I put this…"NO!?"

Before we could move into any place, our furniture, clothing and every other thing in the house needed to be cleaned or pitched. A woman from church asked her "daughter's boyfriend's mom's boyfriend" to do the cleaning. He cleaned two living room chairs first, then moved them over to the church until we needed them.

Day in and day out, we worried about what would come next and about our babies' progress in the hospital. We had a couple of bumps in the road; however, all in all, they were very healthy. The nurses took very good care of them.

One Monday afternoon, on the triplets' twenty-second day at the hospital, when the pediatric doctors made their rounds, we were informed that all three would be ready to go home the next day! I knew we didn't seem as excited as they thought we should be, but by this time we had confided in a couple of nurses that we had grown close to about our circumstances. These few nurses knew how worried and scared we were about leaving the hospital knowing we had no good place to take our babies. We were supposed to be able to take our happy little family home to their newly decorated nursery and live Happily Ever After, but that had been taken from us. Once the doctors left the room, the nurses informed us that we had until midnight of the day of the babies' release to actually take them from the hospital. We could therefore use that time to get things together. However, when our favorite nurse, Joyce, wasn't around, the doctor suggested to us that we stay the night with our babies in the "family ready room" the night before taking them home, in order to get used to it.

That was THE most miserable night of our lives! Oh, the room looked so nice. They really had it set up. There was a TV, a microwave, and a pull-out couch that turned into a bed; and they even provided sheets, blankets and pillows for us.

We never pulled out the bed, to make it up, or turned on the TV. The entire night consisted of getting up with babies because they were wet, or hungry of course, and jumping from the couch to check to make sure they were breathing.

You see, they were all three being sent home on sleep apnea monitors. These monitors were supposed to tell us if and when they stopped breathing, which is very common in premature babies. The monitors they send new parents and babies home with, though, have leads that constantly come off. When this happens, a horrendously loud and annoying beep sounds until you come to check on the baby. Imagine THREE of those going off constantly at all hours of the night, but ONLY when the two adults in the room finally fall into some semblance of sleep!

The next morning, when the other nurses returned to duty, they became hopping mad when they heard about what happened. They said that the doctors NEVER should have put that on us the night before going home, and that we needed all the sleep we could get. They both ordered us to leave and not return until almost midnight. They demanded we go get rest and decide what to do about our living situation.

Tired and weary, Dave and I headed across the street to the Ronald McDonald House. Once there, we discussed what to do. We knew we would not be able to move into the one and only option for an apartment that we had until a week later. I finally went out of our room and found the director of the Ronald McDonald House. I talked to her about our situation, which some of the other workers already knew about. She said that she already knew and that she had talked to others in charge. They decided that since they weren't busy at the moment, we were welcome to stay for a few extra nights WITH the babies.

At a Ronald McDonald House, parents are only permitted to stay in the case that they have a child in the hospital and do not live nearby. Our case had just changed dramatically, in which all three of our children were being released; but unless we wanted to go to a hotel with three one-month-olds, or travel three and a half hours to go to my parents' home, we had nowhere to go! Our friend Toni did offer to let us stay with her and her family, but they really didn't have the room. So, under the circumstances, they allowed us to stay there with the babies.

That next night, Trevor, Abbey and Dylan were officially released from the hospital to the Ronald McDonald House (RMH), room number 3.

FAITH WALK

* **Read Matthew 25:31-46 and Matthew 8:20**

"And Jesus said to him, "Foxes have holes and birds of the air have nests, but the Son of Man has nowhere to lay His head."[1]

* **Have you ever been homeless or known someone who has?**

* **What would your greatest fear be, if you were to lose your home tomorrow?**

Not long ago I took a young man with nowhere to stay to a homeless shelter. It took everything I had within me to not grab him by the arm and run. I didn't want him there. I cried once I left, and most of the way home.

The place was dirty, scary and smelly, and he looked as frightened as I felt.

Since I live in a parsonage and have three small children, I couldn't take him in. It was not a good place, yet there was nowhere else for him to go. It is a scary thing not to have a home, although our situation was very different from that of this young man. Consider volunteering at a homeless shelter or even providing clothing or blankets for a shelter.

---

1   Matthew 8:20 (NKJV)

Chapter 14

TRULY GOING
"HOME"

THE NEXT DAY, MY HUSBAND went to our home to tie up some loose knots and get things going for us to move. He also inquired about getting more of our furniture cleaned.

Once we had found out about the black mold, a friend of mine, Staci, who I had only known for a short time, came and got every single bit of the babies' clothing, sheets, blankets, towels, etc. She took them to her house and washed every piece and kept them for us. She brought me a tote of clothing when we knew they would be released from the hospital so that we would have things for our own children.

That whole first day with my babies totally in my care was an emotional one. I was going on little sleep, lots of worry, and even more heartache. At this point, people that I thought were my friends from our church had not sent one card, or flower, or even come to see us. We had a visit the very first day, and then a couple of weeks after the babies were born. However, even knowing all that we were going through, not one person showed up or even called to comfort or help except for the two friends I've already mentioned. That hurt, and it cut very deep. Fortunately, before we were actually released, another family came up to see us and brought each of the babies a stuffed animal. Abbey still sleeps with "Purple Bear" today.

I think I spent most of that day in tears in the small room at RMH with my three little ones. I would look at them and break out in tears knowing that they were depending on me, and I didn't have much to give! It was breaking me in two! At one point, I needed to go ask something at the front desk, but didn't want to just leave my babies. There was a man whom my husband and I had gotten to know whose daughter was in the hospital. I saw him in the hallway and asked him to just stand there at the door while I ran up front really quickly.

When I poked my head out to the front desk I saw that they were already speaking with someone. I decided that whatever it was that I thought I needed at the time would have to wait. I told them "Never mind," and headed back to my room. Evidently, each of those people that I had just talked to had seen that I had been crying and soon made their way to my room. I sat there on my bed holding a baby, while two or three virtual strangers sat there trying to comfort me and ogled over the babies for a bit. They suggested that I should go to a different room that night, and leave my husband in charge of the babies. What they didn't understand was that I didn't WANT to be separated from my babies; I was just worried about our future. They were just trying to help, but I wouldn't have slept any better in a room by myself.

Around two o'clock that afternoon, someone knocked at my door. I couldn't imagine who it would be, as my parents had already gone home and Dave was up in Michigan trying to take care of things. I answered to find that it was one of the ladies that worked at the RMH.

One of the rules of the RMH was "no food in the rooms", and we had abided by that. However, we hadn't thought about me being in the room all day by myself. Sure, the babies were being fed by me, but I was not being fed in return! I had just kept plugging along and waiting for Dave to come back to us, until this knock on the door.

The woman asked if I had eaten at all today. I told her no, I hadn't, and she said, "Well, we're going to break the rules, and I'm going to go get you something to eat." She went and fixed me a sandwich, fruit and an assortment of other goodies. She made such a nice little lunch for me, that of course, the tears came once again.

She came back a while later and got the tray from me. I had eaten everything on the tray, even the things I didn't normally like, because it all just tasted so good! Then when Dave got back to us that night, I cried some more in his arms.

I called the vice-chairman from the church that was going to see to it that our furniture got steam-cleaned properly, and was told that they would look into it. I hung up. Dave and I got the babies fed, changed and put down for the night so that we could get some rest. Before getting settled in though, there was another knock at our door.

Thereat the door stood our favorite nurse, Joyce. She was sad that she wasn't there to tell us goodbye and see us off, but came in to work to find out that we were all still over at the RMH. We all hugged and she came in to see the babies. She chuckled with love at the fact that the three little ones comfortably fit into one pack and play together. They were sound asleep. She handed us a card, and said that she hoped it helped. We opened it to find a check for one hundred dollars! "Joyce," we said, "that is so not necessary for you to do!"

She assured us that she had talked it over with her husband, and that she had never had a family go through something like this, and wanted to help us in this small way. However, to us, it was helpful in a huge way! We thanked Joyce with another round of hugs and she left to go back to the hospital.

After about three days at the Ronald McDonald House with the babies, we set out for a hotel. That lasted about FIVE minutes! I'm not kidding! We were miserable, the babies were crying, I was crying, and I think Dave was ready to cry! I did what any mother would do–I called MY mommy! I sobbed into the telephone, "Mom, can we just come home? We don't know what else to do? We don't have anywhere to go but a hotel and this just isn't working."

My mom said, "Come home." So we did.

We packed the babies back in the van, and we drove home in the middle of the night. We were five homeless souls, desperate for someone to just take care of us.

My mom and dad had a houseful of family that weekend, so we actually ended up staying with one of my brothers and his wife and girls. I got some of the best sleep I had in a long time. While I stayed there for a few days, Dave went back up to Michigan to try to find us a place to live. I spoke with my friend Staci and she offered to have us come and stay with her until we figured things out. Keep in mind I had only met her a few short months before giving birth, at a "Moms of Multiples" group. Yes, she had multiples also: twin boys that were only eighteen months old. She was insistent that she and her husband wanted us to come and stay with them. So we made the plans for when we came back up to Michigan. For that moment though, I just needed my family. I needed my mommy.

FAITH WALK

* *Read Proverbs 18:24*

* *Has a friend ever let you down?*

* *Have you ever had an 'unlikely friend' come to your rescue?*

* *What does this passage in Proverbs tell us about a Friend?*

People are just that: people. Human. Faulty. When we put our hope or trust in them, we will be disappointed. I have been let down, and I have let others down. There is One, though, that has never let me down.

Chapter 15

EVERYTHING KEEPS FALLING APART

DURING THE TIME THAT WE stayed with my friend Staci and her family, my mom came to clean and pack up our home.

In the meantime, Dave finally found us a place to rent. I went with him to check it out while my mom stayed with the babies. I was not thrilled. It was a three room apartment in the upstairs of an old house. It wasn't going to be ready for another couple of weeks, but we were told it could be ours. I walked twenty steps upstairs and saw it for the first time, and, you guessed it, I wanted to cry. It was starting to seem as though crying was my favorite pastime.

It was not by far the home that I expected to bring my babies into. I wondered how in the world I would ever do anything or go anywhere with the babies by myself with all of those stairs to walk down. There was no way it could be done safely. I would always have to either have help or just be stuck in the house all day.

There were no actual bedrooms in this place, just rooms. And one of the rooms was separated from the other two past the stairs, so Dave, the babies, and I would all have to stay in the two rooms by the kitchen, and the room on the other side of the stairway would have to be a living area, or a "catch all." It was a dark room that didn't interest me much anyway. It was all just depressing, to say the least.

I felt the need to help with the packing up of my own home, so Dave talked to an environmentalist friend of his and asked if it would be ok for us to be in the house as long as we kept windows open. We had found out by this time that the mold was contained in the basement. Since the house didn't have central air, and we wouldn't be using the heat in the middle of the summer, this friend said that it would be ok to be in the house. He instructed that we must keep the windows opened and the air purifier on at all times and insisted that it only be for a week or two.

So, we packed up our things once again, and moved back into this place we had called home for the last year and a half in order to pack up our belongings.

We were there for about a week, and then the apartment would be ready to move into in just three days. No more of our furniture had been steam-cleaned, and we were running out of time. We were already pretty leery of just being in the house, let alone taking everything with us without being cleaned properly. I called the person from our church that had the "friend of a friend" clean the two chairs and asked when we would be able to have the couch and all of our beds cleaned so that we could have a fresh start. The answer I got was, "I haven't seen 'so-n-so' but when I do I'll ask them to ask the other person…" I broke. I told them that "Something is going to have to give. I can't live out of boxes and suitcases anymore. I need a home!"

After we got off of the phone, I went into the living room , where my mom and Dave were with the babies. I was already feeling anxious about having them in this house for a week, and now this! Dave had been suggesting for a couple of weeks at this point that the babies and I should go home with my mom and dad. He would resign and follow us in a couple of weeks. I kept insisting that I didn't want that because we needed to be together. We needed to be a family!

On this particular night as we sat in the living room and I told them about the phone conversation through my tears, Dave once again suggested his plan. Once more I said no, but as we sat there, I finally just handed off the baby I had been holding and said, "I'll be back."

Dave and Mom asked where I was going, but I didn't really know what to tell them. I simply told them, "I don't know. I just need to go for a drive. I promise I'll be ok, and that I'll be right back. I just need to do this."

So I grabbed the van keys and I left. I only drove a mile or so down the street to another church much bigger than ours with an even bigger parking lot. I parked in the very back of the lot, stopped the van, and screamed my head off! I cried and I prayed, and I begged God to show me "Why! Why is this happening to us NOW!?" I screamed and cried out to God until I had to open the van door and be sick in that parking lot.

Then I drove home. I took Trevor back into my arms, and when Dave once again suggested that he resign, and that the babies and I go with Mom and Dad and he would follow in two weeks, I simply said, "OK." That was that.

The next day, Mom and Dad and I packed up what the babies and I needed and we left. We lost the deposit on the apartment, but I just couldn't do it. Leaving Dave was the last thing I wanted, but it had to be done for our health and sanity.

This was the beginning of September in 2001. So one morning while I was feeding the babies, I turned on the TV to see the second plane crash into the Twin Towers in New York City. Like everyone else in America, I was devastated. As the news continued and more of the horrific details came out, I had thoughts of never seeing my husband again! I wondered if we would be at war and if it would be impossible for him to get to me or me to him. Of course that was not the case, and he was with us in two weeks like we had planned. What a sad month September turned out to be.

Through our entire stay at Ronald McDonald and on into the circumstances that followed, I had started to make a certain song my daily prayer. It's a song I had always known and loved, but it became dear to my heart during this time. I think it was more of a reminder to me than anything else. For the first time in my life, the words meant something to me. Every morning as I got ready to go see the babies in the NICU, or got up in the middle of the night no matter where we were, I sang this song to myself and the babies over and over, most of the time in tears…

> *When peace like a river attendeth my way*
> *When sorrows like sea billows roll,*
> *Whatever my lot, Thou has taught me to say*
> *It is well; it is well, with my soul.*

This next verse really brings out the tears in me:

> *Though Satan should buffet, though trials should come,*
> *Let THIS blessed assurance control;*
> *That Christ has regarded my helpless estate,*
> *And has shed His own blood for my soul!*
> *It is well with my soul. It is well; it is well with my soul!*[1]

---

1   It is Well With My Soul, H. G. Spafford

During this time apart, Dave asked me to start looking in the paper for a place for us to rent. I kept arguing with him about that, because I didn't see how in the world we could afford anything! Yes, he was working for two weeks and then we would have two weeks' vacation pay still coming, but the pay we were receiving at the church at that time was only about $250.00 a week, and would not get us very far. I put it off for as long as I could, and then he insisted that I look for something. I started looking, but as I expected, there wasn't much we could afford on our "good looks" alone.

Where had my faith gone? Where was the faith that I had when I proclaimed to the God of the universe that I knew if there was only one baby in me, He could turn it into two? Where was the faith that I had when I knew that all of my babies would be fine and healthy, and then I saw that happen right before my eyes? Oh, we of little faith.

FAITH WALK

* *Read James 1*

* *According to this chapter, what do our trials do for our faith?*

* *What does the Lord promise us if we endure our trials?*

God allows us to be tempted, but does not tempt. He doesn't play games. That's Satan's job.

There were times up to this point in my story in which people would say to me, "It's time for something good to come your way. You've been through so much. More than a person should have to go through."

My response to that was, "I have had something good come my way. Something marvelous and miraculous! I have three little babies that by the doctors' own words weren't expected to be healthy or even live! I have a husband that came into my life through fairytale circumstances! In addition, I have my health, when only a short time ago, I thought I may not have my life! If God has brought us through everything so far, He will continue to bring us through this time.

Life is hard, but do not give up on God. Keep believing (faith) that He has a plan.

Chapter 16

GOD DOES WORK IN MYSTERIOUS WAYS

BEFORE DAVE EVEN FINISHED OUT his two weeks and came to Mom and Dad's house, I found a place that was a possibility. It was about forty-five minutes from their house, but it was in a nice little town near Amish Country. I called the number and asked about the house. It had two bedrooms, which is all we would need at this point, and a nice backyard. It was affordable, and so I set up a day to go see it.

The man who owned the house said he just couldn't meet me on Sunday unless it was after church. I told him I would rather not meet Sunday, and then we talked about the fact that we were both Christians. We planned to meet on Monday of the following week.

Mom and the babies and I went down to see the house. I explained our situation to the property owner, and the fact that he would probably see when he did the credit check that we'd been late on bills but had always caught up. We really needed our own place to live and to be a family. He told me that he had lost his wife and that they owned a few houses, but since her death, he decided to sell them. However, he was having some trouble selling this one and had decided to go ahead and rent it. Then he told me, "I have to tell you why I'm having trouble before I can rent it to you though. I just wouldn't feel right otherwise."

"OK," I said, feeling a little anxious about it now. Then he proceeded to tell me that just about six months prior, there had been a man and woman renting the house. The man had a drug problem and he apparently beat his wife.

"He was murdered in this house. His wife shot him," he told me.

I just looked at him and said, "Well, I'm not afraid of ghosts. I do not believe in them. Just don't tell me what room or where it happened and we have a deal."

He agreed, and said that he was willing to rent it to us even though we didn't have a steady income.

I signed the lease, and we went back to Mom and Dad's house. I could not wait to tell Dave about it. I called him when we got back and explained the situation. He wasn't too thrilled after hearing about the shooting, but I explained that beggars couldn't be choosers, and he agreed.

Dave finally finished his two weeks and came down to be with us. He signed up with a temp-agency working security jobs. We decided that Mom and I would spend time going down to the house and getting cribs set up and the house in order before we actually moved in. However, before we could do anything, the property owner called me.

"I'm so sorry. I don't know how to tell you this, but remember I told you I had had the house for sale, but since it didn't sell, I decided to rent?"

"Yes," I answered.

"Well, I have a buyer. I actually told the realtor I don't want to sell now, because I have already promised the place to you, but she said I cannot get out of it now and that I have to sell it to this buyer. I am so sorry. I did everything I could to get out of it," he told me.

I told him that I was disappointed but I understood. I appreciated his trying to get out of it just for us. I told him, "Not everyone would do something like that. Thank you." And we hung up.

I told Dave and my mom and dad, and we all agreed that God would work things out. Until then we had a roof over our heads.

A few days later though, Ned the property owner called me again!

"Julie," he said, "I have great news! If you're still interested you can have the house!"

"YES," I answered, "I most definitely am still interested."

I asked him what happened, and he explained that a man was buying the house for his daughter and requested a "flood report." Ned told me that even though the house had never been flooded as far back as they could find, the man said he didn't want the house because it was possible.

If that wasn't God, I don't know what it was! We spent a few weeks getting things exactly the way we wanted them, and then we moved in. It seemed as though maybe we did rent on our "good looks" alone!

We had a nice little home. I applied for government assistance since Dave was still only working through the temp-agency at this point. With the assistance we received, we were able to have more than enough food on our table. It was rent and the other expenses we were struggling with. However, somehow, God was providing, and we were surviving.

FAITH WALK

* ***Read Psalm 56***

No matter what situation you find yourself in as you're reading this book, God knows *every single detail*. He knows what you're feeling and thinking. In Psalm 56:8, we learn that God actually keeps track of all of our sorrows, and collects our tears in a bottle. Wow, I don't know about you, but *I* don't even remember all of the times I've cried. Yet, God keeps track of every single tear! Someone that cares that much is not going to let us down. Take your sorrows to Him, and talk them over. He *will* show you what to do.

Chapter 17

BEING FED
IN THE DESERT

ONE OF MY BEST FRIENDS, Lynn, called me one day and said, "Do you at least have television to watch when the babies are sleeping?" She was worried about me being alone all day while Dave was at work and I was home taking care of the babies. I told her no, we couldn't afford to get cable, and that was the only way we could get any stations, but that I was ok. When the babies slept, I was sleeping, and so it wasn't so bad.

She called back later to tell me that her husband said that they were sending the cable company to hook up some TV for us—for me. That was just the beginning of the love and support we received from them and others that year.

Dave and I were told not to take the babies out a lot and to keep them out of church and large crowds for several months. Therefore, we took turns going to churches to find one to attend. One Sunday morning Dave would go somewhere, and then I would go somewhere else or the same place that night. Then the next Sunday I would go in the morning, and he would go in the evening. We found a doctor we liked for the whole family, and he just happened to be a Christian also! We visited the church he went to several times, and the Wesleyan church nearby. Those were our two favorites.

We plowed along like this for a while, until one Sunday afternoon my mom and dad called to ask us to meet them for lunch. We hadn't been anywhere as a family yet, since the babies were so small and we didn't have the money. Dad asked us to come and he would pay for our dinners. We were so excited to go out as a family, we could hardly wait.

We got everything that the babies would need and everyone packed into the van, and took off. Soon into the trip, we realized we were lost. I called the restaurant and asked them to get my dad. He came to the phone and I explained where we were. After talking to him, we realized that we were about forty-five minutes in the wrong direction. We knew that everyone else was already there and would have a long wait ahead of them if they had to wait for us, so we told them to eat without us. I hoped that we could all do it another time.

For some reason, this broke us both. When we got back home and got the babies settled in, Dave and I both just broke down. I don't remember what was said, I just remember Dave standing in a doorway, and I watched him cry for the first time in all of this mess. Then I started to cry, and felt like I couldn't be "low" enough, so I dropped to the floor from the couch, fell to my face, and sobbed.

I'll have you know that this all had nothing to do with actually missing dinner. I think it was that everything hit us in that moment. We had been through so much in the last couple of years with my illness, then the babies, and the mold, that when we got an invitation to go out and be with family, it lifted our spirits. However, to end up at home without having seen the family, let alone having the money to get a hamburger, made us both feel low. So we broke. We knew that the babies were in God's plan, but for some reason, nothing was going right ever since we had had them!

Christmastime came, and we had absolutely no money for Christmas gifts. Of course, the babies were only five months old, and not able to even know anything about Christmas or gifts. But their mommy and daddy knew. We hadn't really been able to buy any toys, or anything "fun" for that matter up to that point, so we were down about not being able to Christmas shop for our new trio!

Then I had a marvelous idea! With the five showers that we had been given, we had a pretty good supply of diapers! We had an entire closet full of diapers, to be exact. We knew we would use them all, except the preemie ones. We had been given a load of preemie diapers, but by the time the babies came out of the hospital, they were in newborn diapers. So, I packed up all of those preemie diapers, and took them to Baby's R Us. They let me exchange them for anything in the store.

Right or wrong, responsible or not, I was able to Christmas shop for my babies and get them several little baby toys each for the exchange of those diapers! Never let it be said that a mother isn't resourceful when it comes to her children!

We packed up and went home to Mom and Dad's for a few days for Christmas. We had such fun and a nice time seeing everyone. The family was in awe of the triplets, and it was exciting to show them off. For a few days, we forgot about the struggles we faced financially and just enjoyed family.

The day after Christmas, we went back to our new little home. Dave went up to unlock the door before getting the babies and me out of the van. When he came back to us, he had an odd look on his face.

"I found this envelope in the door," he said, and then he asked me, "What would you say if I told you that someone left us a hundred dollars!"

I got all excited and said, "No way! Who would do that?"

He told me, "It's from the Nazarene church. That's the same one that our doctor goes to!"

I was in awe and disbelief. "You know he had something to do with that. They don't even know us! We've only visited there a couple of times, and not even together!"

Dave said, "Yes, I know. It had to be the doctor, but it's also not a hundred."

"What?" I asked. "But you just said…"

He said, "Yes, I know. I asked what you would think if I told you someone left us a hundred dollars, but it's not a hundred…it's a THOUSAND dollars!"

"What?" I sobbed. "Are you kidding me?"

He wouldn't have kidded about something like that. Sure enough, our doctor's church gave us a thousand-dollar gift for Christmas!

A month later, unexpectedly, my friend Lynn Minner called again. She said she wanted to know the name of my property owner.

I honestly couldn't imagine why in the world she would need his name! I told her, but then I quickly racked my brain trying to figure out why she asked what she did next! "Could I have his address?"

"Now why in the world would you want my landlord's address?"

"That's for me to know," she said.

I told her that after everything we'd been through, I'd like to know why. I couldn't honestly imagine why. I really couldn't!

She told me, "Well, because Jeff (her husband) and I want to pay your rent!"

I said, "What? Are you serious? For when, January?"

Then she told me, "For as long as you need it until you don't need us to anymore."

Wow. I thought after the last six months that I didn't have any more tears, but I did. These friends paid our rent for us for the next several months. Almost the entire time we lived in that house, they paid for it.

FAITH WALK

* ***Read Exodus 16***

When we are wandering in a desert, it's easy to give in to fear. The uncertainty of our tomorrows can weigh heavily on our hearts and cause us to start questioning our decisions, our faith and God Himself! When was a time that you were in a desert, unable to see clearly to tomorrow?

* ***What did the Israelites complain about to Moses in this chapter in Exodus?***

* ***God gave specific instructions on how to handle the manna that He sent to them. What where those instructions?***

"Lord, help us to follow Your instructions as we face the deserts of life. When we no longer know how to put one foot in front of the other, take us by the hand and lead. Let us not complain about what we don't have, but rejoice in what we do have. Above all, remind us always that what we have is only because of You. In Jesus' Name, Amen!"

Chapter 18

SECOND CLASS
CITIZEN?

UNFORTUNATELY, THAT SAME MONTH, JANUARY, Dave's Gramma died. Neither Dave's mom nor Gramma had wanted a big funeral. They only wanted a simple graveside service with family. So, that's what we did. In the middle of January, Dave and my mom and dad and sister stood beside her grave, just as we did for his mom, and had a small committal service. My sister and I sang, Dave said a few words, we prayed, and that was it. After 94 years of life, (74 for his mom) it was now over.

Not long after Gramma's funeral, I became sick again while I was at home in the house we were renting. I was alone with the babies and Dave was working at one of the temporary jobs he had been given. I went into the bathroom.

The next thing I knew, I was waking up on the floor sandwiched in between the commode and the tub, with a bump on my forehead! This particular time really scared me. What if I had been holding one of the babies when this happened?

When Dave came home, I told him what had happened, and how worried I was. When it happened before, I had been pregnant, and they "chalked" it up to the pregnancy, with the hormones and blood pressure, etc. However, I was now no longer pregnant, so why in the world was this still happening? We needed to find out. I had seven-month-old triplets to take care of!

Also during this time, our family doctor was trying to help us find a specialist for me because of the Crohn's Disease. I needed to have a gastroenterologist in order to help manage the disease. Unfortunately, there were none in the area.

However, there were a couple general surgeons in the area that also did colonoscopies. My doctor thought that maybe they could take care of me. It was such a small town that nobody there really understood what I needed. I did go to see one of those two general surgeons, and he did perform the colonoscopy, but then he suggested that I travel to the next big city to see a specialist because of how progressed my illness was. It was more than he was willing or able to handle. He referred me to a woman specialist, and made an appointment for me there.

The time came for me to go see this specialist, and I was a little excited. In the past, I had only had male specialists, and this time would have someone I felt would understand my needs as a woman better. I arrived at her office and was taken into a room. It was in this room that I sat and sat and sat. I waited for quite some time for this doctor to come see me. When she did come in, I lost all hope that this would be a pleasant visit. She didn't bother to smile at me and barely introduced herself, nor did she bother to shake my hand. She sat down and commanded the nurse that was there to stay where she was, as she wanted someone else in the room. I knew by the apologetic look on the nurse's face that this would not be pleasant. She then began to ask questions about my disease and when and where I had last been seen and by whom. She wasted about fifteen minutes of her time, and an hour of mine considering travel time and the time it took for me to wait for her, because when she was done, this is what she told me: "I will consider this a consultation, but I will not be seeing you as a patient. You are already established with this other doctor, and I will not be taking you in."

I explained to her that he was not actually what I needed and he himself knew that, which was why he was sending me to her. However, she didn't want to hear it. It finally became known, that she did not take patients that were low enough on the American totem pole to be on government assistance...Medicaid.

I left that office so humiliated and angry that I couldn't wait to leave and never look back. I went to the surgeon and explained to him how horrible this woman was and about the way, she had treated me because I was on assistance. I told him that she didn't give me a chance to explain why I was, and what we had been through.

"She couldn't get me out of her office fast enough!" I told him.

I don't think he believed it was *that* bad at first, but then he called her right in front of me. When he hung up, he told me he was sorry, and he would be finding another doctor for me.

A couple of weeks later, I ended up at the best gastroenterologist office I could have ever asked for! The new office had two doctors in it who were so kind and well-educated that they completely outshone this other woman doctor in every way.

One of them was a former doctor with the White House staff, and the other a former doctor with the Navy! They started me on a new medication called Immuran, which is an immunosuppressant drug. It's used with autoimmune diseases (in which the immune system fights itself), which is what Crohn's Disease is classified as. By suppressing the immune system, inflammation is reduced. Crohn's Disease is inflammation in the gastrointestinal tract, but from there it causes all sorts of other problems within the body. My new doctors were hoping to slow down the disease with the Immuran, because so far, I had not had any worthwhile remissions.

I was willing to do whatever it took, because I knew that I needed to be stronger for my babies.

FAITH WALK

* *Read James 2*

* *Have you ever been judged solely on your appearance, "social standing" or lack thereof?*

* *How does it feel to be judged?*

* *According to this chapter in James, what does God think about "playing favorites," so to speak?*

I was humiliated the day I walked out of that doctor's office. I wanted to lash out, so as I left, I slammed the door as hard as I possibly could. She looked at me with such contempt, yet she had no idea who I really was or where I had come from. She didn't know what I had been through or was going through at the time. I can still see the look on the nurse's face as she stood by and listened to the conversation. I could tell she was embarrassed and would have rather been anywhere else but there. What would cause a well-educated doctor, who took an oath to "first, do no harm", to act in such a way? Ignorance.

As you go through your everyday life, try to look upon people the way God sees them. Actually pray and ask God to give you that insight. You'll be amazed at how you start seeing others.

Chapter 19

FROM BAD
TO WORSE

I WAS STILL PASSING OUT whenever I became ill. I spoke to our family doctor again and told him about it. He said that there were a few tests we could run, but thought that it was a bit premature to get worried about. He thought that as long as I was feeling better, that it was nothing to worry about and probably still just a hormone from the pregnancy.

However, at the end of March, it happened again. This time I fell on the floor of the dining room, just a few feet away from our babies playing on the living room floor. I called the doctor and made an appointment. We went ahead and planned to start getting some tests done.

Around that time, we received word that Dave's dad had died. I had never met his father. I felt sad that there was never a chance for the babies or myself to meet the man who played a huge part in bringing my husband into the world!

In the midst of it all, Dave's brother and nephew had planned a trip to Ohio to not only meet me for the first time, but also to see the babies and take care of some things that needed to be done after the deaths of Mom and Gramma.

Unfortunately, in the days leading up to their arrival, I began to feel sicker and sicker. Let me tell you about the day they were to arrive. I literally pushed myself to the brink that day, and still did not get everything accomplished that I wanted to. Had my mom not just had knee surgery, I'm sure she would have come to help me, but she was laid up with her own set of physical problems.

I never got the dishes done, so I threatened Dave that if he let his brother and nephew go anywhere near our kitchen, I would not be responsible for my own actions! I tidied up as best I could everywhere else, and since we had such a small place, we got them a motel room, which was close by.

Dave went to the airport to meet their flight, and I knew I had a little time, so I put the babies in their baby swings and I lay down on the couch. I felt so sick to my stomach that I surprised myself when I woke up from a little catnap! I felt so peaceful in those few minutes. With the sound of three baby swings going, I was just lulled to rest! The peace ended quickly though. My first mistake was opening my eyes. My second mistake was actually looking over at the babies. Two were sleeping, and one was looking straight at me. Trevor was swinging in his swing peacefully, but when he made eye contact with me, he let me know clearly that he was ready to get out of that contraption!

He began to cry, so I started to get up from the couch. I couldn't move. No, not because I was tired or worn out or sick, although I was all of those things, but because I literally could not move! My back was suddenly in so much pain, it felt as though something inside were breaking! As I struggled to get up from the couch one way or another, Trevor's cries turned into wails, and soon the other two babies were waking. Finally, I rolled off the couch, because no other regular method was working! His swing, of course, had to be the furthest one from me, so I proceeded to crawl across the living room towards him. I tried calming him down by speaking to him as I crawled, but nothing was going to make him happy. Nothing, that is, except me getting there and getting him out!

I finally got to him, rose up on my knees, and reached for him. "AAHH!" I moaned, and then I truly began to cry! I couldn't even begin to lift him out! I tried repeatedly. Finally, I was sobbing, Trevor was sobbing, and the other two were starting to get so annoyed with us for waking them up this way, that they started to cry too!

Ultimately, I had to sit on the floor, grab Trevor, and let him fall to the floor with my assistance. My arms would not let me lift! My back was stopping me from doing any upward movements of my arms. I prayed and said, "God, help us." I dragged him out of his swing and across the floor to my lap. We didn't have cell phones at the time; consequently, in order to get back to the phone by the couch and get somewhere where I could have something to lean against, we needed to make our way back across the living room together. I tucked Trevor under one arm like a football and crawled to a spot on the floor by the couch. We sat there for a moment with him still crying, but not as badly, and me wincing in pain. It was as though I had just pulled us both out of a dangerous situation in the desert-dodging rattlesnakes! I was exhausted and in pain, and I just wanted the day to be over!

I called my mom and dad in tears and asked them to pray for me. I explained what had just happened, and that I still could not move. I told them that I had just taken some pain medications, and asked if they would pray that they would soon kick in, so that I could not only feed and take care of my babies, but that I would also be able to greet my in-laws when they arrived.

Of course, my mom said, "We're on our way!"

Normally I would have sobbed out an "OK," but this time I knew I couldn't let them do that. If I had a virus, I didn't want Mom to get sick and get an infection. In addition, it just wasn't fair, because she needed to be resting her knee, so it would be selfish of me to have them come. I knew Dave would be back soon, and I told them so. I asked them to just pray "right now" and then we hung up.

After a few minutes of sitting there with Trevor and all four of us having a good cry, the medicine kicked in, and I was able to get all three dressed and fed before Dave arrived home with his family.

Somehow, by strength that was not my own, I made it through that evening, and I even ate a piece of pizza with everyone! I wanted to feel better and just have a great time with Dave's brother and nephew, and although I made it through without incident, I wasn't myself. As soon as they left to go to their hotel for the evening, I couldn't wait to get into bed. I had a doctor's appointment the next day, and I could hardly wait! I didn't have time to be sick. I had nine-month-old babies who were becoming very active and needed me to be active also!

FAITH WALK

* ***Read 2 Kings 20:1-11***

In verses 1-3 Hezekiah learns that he will not recover and that his illness will not get better. He's told he will die from it. In verse 3 Hezekiah says to God , " 'Remember, O Lord, how I have always tried to be faithful to you and do what is pleasing in your sight.'– Then he broke down and wept."

Wow, I can *so* relate to poor Hezekiah! Can you?

Have you ever been extremely ill unto death? Maybe you or someone you love has a disease like mine, or cancer, or AIDS, or some other illness that tends to scare the socks off of us. If that's the case, we know exactly how Hezekiah felt.

What made God change His mind? What did He do for Hezekiah?

When we are sick and dying, let us turn to God for peace and comfort. Let us trust in Him.

Chapter 20

SOMETHING IS NOT RIGHT

THAT NIGHT WAS HORRIBLE. SINCE I was up all night and feeling sick and miserable, Dave got up with the babies so that I could rest as much as possible. Unfortunately, there wasn't much resting possible!

The next day when I went to my appointment, the doctor saw me, talked with me, and told me to do the "B.R.A.T." diet and get plenty of liquids. A B.R.A.T. diet consists of Bananas, Rice, Apples or Applesauce and Toast. He then told me that if I got worse over the weekend, since this was a Friday, to go into the Emergency Room at the hospital. He also wanted to start doing some tests because of the issue with passing out. He asked one of the nurses to draw some blood, and he set up a C.A.T. scan for the following week. He wanted to have a mobile heart monitor on me, but said we would wait until I was feeling better to do both of those things.

The nurse wasn't able to draw any blood because I was so dehydrated. After attempting at least six times with no results, she sent me home. I was supposed to come back Monday and try again, after I was "feeling better." Sad to say, we never got to those blood tests or any of the other tests that our doctor wanted to do.

I went home that day, feeling so drained that all I wanted to do was sleep. Unfortunately, when I got home, Dave and his brother informed me that they needed to go take care of some paperwork so that our nephew could have his grandmother's car. The men and our fifteen-year-old nephew left for just a bit, and I sat with the babies in the living room.

I remember sitting on the couch, once again with poor Trevor beside me. Yes, I set my small nine-month-old baby beside me, because by the time I got him and me to the couch, I didn't have enough energy in my arms to lift him up to my lap. I set him in the crook of my arm on the couch, and stared into space. The other two babies were sleeping, so the two of us sat there and waited until the men came back home.

When they got back, I told Dave that I needed to go lay down, and that I "didn't feel right." He explained that he and his brother still needed to go somewhere, not truly realizing how sick I was becoming. Then again, I didn't understand how bad it was getting either. Don't forget that when he married me, he married a sick woman, and I had been through many flare-ups with the Crohn's and him right beside me. I was sure this flare would soon pass also, and life would go back to normal just as it always had. At this point in our lives and marriage, we thought that's what would happen; things would calm down once again, and we would go on with life.

So, for him and his brother to do what they needed to do, they left our fifteen-year-old nephew, who had never been around a baby in his life, let alone three babies, to help me while they were gone. They promised not to be long, and they left. I told Erik, our nephew, that I was sorry to do this to him, but that I just couldn't function. He was such a good sport about it all. I told him that I would be in the very next room sleeping, but that if he needed me for anything, to come get me. I don't know how long it was, because to me it seemed like an eternity, but he never once came to get me. He fed the babies, changed diapers, and gave them their overall care, and he did it all by himself for the very first time in his life, without ever disturbing his Aunt Julie.

I, however, lay in the next room sicker than I had ever been in my life, not realizing that I was near death.

I remember how I felt like it was yesterday. I would feel such fear, and then I would actually hear an audible voice, that at the time I thought was Dave, tell me to "wake up." I would turn slowly in my bed, only to see that no one was there. I felt that I was moving in slow motion, and I actually probably was. I couldn't stand up out of my bed to go to the bathroom because my back hurt so badly I couldn't straighten up. I tossed and turned and wanted nothing more than to just sleep! There was only one thing that stopped me from falling asleep, and that was God Himself. I remember thinking that I needed to sleep. But then I would panic and realize that if I fell asleep, somehow I knew that I would not wake up. Then I would argue with myself because I was so tired, and tell myself, "Sleep! If you die, you die! Even THAT would be better than this is!"

Then, I would think about my babies, and Dave and my parents and friends and family. Those thoughts would keep me awake for a few minutes, but then I would get so exhausted from trying to stay awake. Every time, as I would start to fall asleep again, I would hear that whisper in my ear, again thinking that Dave was home and talking to me: "Get up!" Then I would open my eyes to see that he wasn't there after all.

At one point I felt that I was going to be physically ill, but

I knew I wouldn't be able to stand up because of my back. So, with every ounce of strength in me, I pulled myself in a half circle around my bed until I was leaning off of the end of the bed. I found a bag to get sick in, left it there, and then pulled myself back around to my pillows. After that, I lay there and cried. I knew that I was in big trouble, but there was nothing I could do. With my teenage nephew, three babies and no car there to get me anywhere, I was stuck! I wanted to call out to Erik in the next room and have him call 911, but I didn't even have the strength to speak, let alone yell. No matter how hard I tried, nothing would work.

When Dave finally did get home, I asked him if he had already been home once and came in to check on me. He said that he had not, and I argued with him for a few minutes insisting that he had at least opened the bedroom door and asked me how I was! He said, "No, honey, this is the first time I've been home!"

I said, "No, I heard you out there and was kind of upset that you weren't coming in to check on me."

He told me, "Honey, I just got home, and I came straight in here to check on you!"

I knew I wasn't making any sense, and he must have thought I was still half asleep. I really was delusional.

I was told years later that my nephew wasn't alone the entire time, and that my brother-in-law was there for part of it. For the longest time, I had no clue!

That night, I called to Dave to come help me get up to go to the bathroom. It took the two of us ten minutes to get me out of bed because my back hurt so badly. It felt like something was breaking in my spine.

I went into the bathroom and I noticed that I was developing a funny looking rash all over my legs. Then I looked in the mirror and realized it was on my neck and arms as well!

It then dawned on me that a couple of days before, I had been on the phone with my mom when I noticed a bruised-looking spot on my shin. I remembered telling her that I didn't know how it got there, and that the oddest thing was that it didn't even hurt! As I investigated further, this "bruise" was spreading, and I had several of them all over my shins! Two different skin "disorders" were now on my body that was physically unable to function anymore. I was starting to get worried.

Dave was in the kitchen doing all of those dishes that had been sitting there since his brother and nephew had arrived two days before, and I sat down in a chair and asked for a glass of water.

I drained that glass, and begged for another. Then I drank that glass and asked him for another one. I was so thirsty, I felt almost panicky if he didn't get more water for me right away! Finally, I told him that I thought I should go to the hospital. We were in a quandary though, because he would have to stay with the babies, but who would go with me?

Dave called and had my dad come. As we walked out to the car that night it was snowing and I could hardly stand on my own two feet!

Now, you need to picture my dad. He built tires for many years back in his twenties and thirties. He was always a big, strong guy to me! However, due to his job, he injured his back when I was a teenager, and had to have back surgery. Ever since that time, he never was able to feel his feet again. That's right, no feeling whatsoever in his feet.

At the time I'm writing this, my dad can hardly stand. He has a hard time balancing, because he can't feel his feet or his lower legs because of a neuropathy due to the back injury years ago.

On our wedding day, it took so long for our friend who married us to get to the "who gives this woman," part, that I was holding my dad up by the time he was finally able to blurt out, "Her mother and I!", and sit back down!

The night he came to take me to the hospital, he was somewhere in between not being able to feel his feet, and not being able to feel the lower parts of his legs anymore.

As you may imagine, we were quite a sight trying to walk out to his car together, neither of us being able to stand on our own two feet and both of us leaning on each other. We laugh about it now, wondering how in the world we did it. Why didn't we just call an ambulance and have Dad meet me at the hospital?

FAITH WALK

* ***Read Job***

Yes, that's right, read the book of Job sometime! I have no idea what specific book, chapter or verse I would pick for this Faith Walk. I simply know that Job is who I felt like. I was literally falling apart at the seams.

I don't think I had ever been so scared of my own body, and trust me, my body can be frightening in the right lighting! Here lay my three precious babies, and I'm heading to the hospital wondering what in the world was happening to me. My poor babies. That's all I could think of.

Has life come crashing around you lately? Read Job.

Chapter 21

24 HOURS

ONCE WE GOT TO THE hospital, it wasn't any better. Since it was in the middle of a cold winter night, there weren't many hospital personnel or patients there. When Dad pulled up in front of the door, I looked at him and said, "Dad, I don't think I can make it!"

Dad looked at me and said, "I don't know if I can make it either…but I'll try!"

So he went in and got a nurse, who came out with a wheelchair.

When they took my temperature, we were all able to understand why I could barely stand on my own two feet. I had a temperature of 105.5.

They took me to a room immediately and got a doctor to come see me right away. We found out also that my potassium was dangerously low, which probably explained the severe pain in my back.

I thought, "OK, they'll give me something to make me feel better, give me something for these TWO rashes that are developing on my arms and legs, and I'll go home and finally get some sleep!"

However, when the doctor came back into the room, he told me that he wanted to keep me overnight, because he wasn't sure what the problem was. He said he already conferred with another doctor, and they agreed that I needed to be admitted to the hospital. My heart sunk. I looked at Dad and cried. Dad called Dave for me and explained to him that they wanted to keep me overnight t We all thought that I would be going home the next morning, but we were wrong.

When they first took me to a room, they quarantined me. No one was to come into my room unless they had on a gown, gloves, and mask. I've had many horrible feelings in my life, and I've had times in which I felt like an outcast. However, nothing compares to being put into a room and being told that you aren't allowed to go to the bathroom or get out of bed without help, and then that "help" has to be covered from head to toe just to be near you!

Now, at this point in this story, you've gotten to know me pretty well. Therefore, I'm not afraid or embarrassed to tell you that when a person with Crohn's Disease is sick, it's next to IMPOSSIBLE for them to wait for a nurse even on a good day in order to be helped to the bathroom. Try having Crohn's Disease, being in the midst of a flare/unknown illness, waiting for a nurse, and then waiting for said nurse to get gowned up! Then imagine said nurse coming in, and saying, "Oops, there's no bed pan in here! I'll be right back!"

"Noooooooooooo!"

Anyway, they soon decided, after I argued and begged them, that I could finally get up to go to the bathroom as long as someone was there to go with me. I got up to sneak there on my own once, when I was caught and scolded, so I never tried that again. It also wasn't long before they realized that whatever was going on with me was just with me, and that they didn't need to be covered up like they were going to see E.T. in order to assist me. That was a relief!

The next morning, our family doctor came in to visit me. He informed me that he was going to let the doctor that had been assigned to me at the hospital take care of me, and that he was just there to see how I was doing. I didn't realize it then, but later I came to understand that he now saw how sick I had become. He wanted this doctor, who was an internalist, to take care of me, because of all that was happening to my body.

He told me, though, that he realized he should have done more and that he should have at least prayed with me when I was in his office the day before. So right there by my hospital bedside, he prayed for God to heal me.

The hospital doctor said that since I was going to be having some tests done because of the issue of passing out, that while I was in, they might as well do an MRI on me. They scratched the CAT scan, and took me to have an MRI.

When I got back from that, they moved me to a different room. In this room, I was able to be visited without feeling like I was an extra terrestrial from outer space! Although I didn't feel much better, just being in a room where other living beings were nearby, and having my dad back to be with me, made me feel so much better.

As I came back from the first of many tests that were run, I saw the original general surgeon who had referred me to the woman who had treated me so badly. They had called for him to come take a biopsy of the rash that was on my arms and upper body. When he saw that it was me, he apologized profusely for ever sending me to the doctor that had turned me away. He said that she sent him a "two page dissertation on how to send patients to her in the future."

He then told me he would never be sending any more patients to her again! I seem to have a knack for getting the doctors that no one wants to send anyone else to after they've seen me. Watch out, docs!

This doctor, though, came to my bedside, spoke kindly, and told me what he would be doing on the following day for the biopsy. He then wished me a good night. Soon after that, my dad also wished me a good night, and went home.

I turned out the lights and tried to get some sleep and not think of my sick stomach or odd rashes on my body. I tried not to think of the babies at home that needed their mommy and were not getting me. I tried not to think of the times of feeding and holding that I was missing by being at the hospital. I tried to just go to sleep.

Then the nurse came in to see if I was awake because the doctor from the hospital was on the phone and wanted to speak with me.

I thought that was somewhat odd, but I picked up the phone and answered. Sure enough, it was the internalist doctor, and he said that the MRI results had been read and he had just received word from the radiologist. I could tell he was at a restaurant or some such place, and wondered why he was calling me if he was out to dinner with his family!

While I was having these thoughts, he was talking, and then it sunk in. He was calling because it wasn't good. I heard the words "brain mass" and "possible tumor", and more commotion in the background. Then he said, "We will be transferring you tonight to another hospital to see a neurosurgeon. Now I'm not saying you will need surgery, but there is definitely something there. Do you want to call your husband or do you want me to call him for you?"

I was stunned. I was all alone now; everyone had gone. I asked him, "Could you please call my husband? I don't want to be the one to tell him this."

I hung up the phone, and threw up. Within 24 hours, my world had turned upside down.

FAITH WALK

* ***Read Jeremiah 31:1-14***

Get Up and Walk, that's the name of the book. I feel like the last few chapters have been real "downers," but this was my life! I'm sure you too have gone through seasons in which everything seemed to keep getting worse. Up to this point in the book, it was around April of 2002. Dave and I had only been married since June of '99. This was a lot of heartache and trials in a very short time.

God's promise to Israel in this passage from Jeremiah is our promise too. Verse 13 says, "The young women will dance for joy, and the men—old and young—will join in the celebration. I will turn their mourning into joy. I will comfort them and exchange their sorrow for rejoicing."

When everything seems to go from bad to worse with no end in sight, dwell upon the words of this verse, because joy *does* come in the morning!

Chapter 22

FINDING GOD
IN A 'PRISON CELL'

So cold. That's what I remember of the ambulance ride to the next hospital. They took my temperature and it was high again, and all I could do was shiver. I kept begging everyone for blankets, but of course, they didn't want to give me any so that my fever would break. Yes, it was cold outside, but I just couldn't get enough blankets on me! I was freezing! By the time I got to the next hospital in the middle of the night, my dad had gotten a call from Dave, and was there to meet me in my new room. My new prison cell. I remember thinking it looked more like a prison cell than a hospital room.

As the nurses turned me, cajoled me, jostled me, and hooked things up to me, my fever broke and I became unbearably hot! Even though it was freezing outside, I asked them to turn my air conditioning on! The fever had been so high, that after it broke, my sheets were soaked with perspiration and had to be changed. After all was said and done, and the fury of nurses and buttons and beepers had left the room, my dad and I were all that were left.

I was terribly scared. But I was also so emotionally and physically drained that I just wanted to sleep and be left alone by anyone wearing white! Before Dad left again for the second time in one night, he said to me: "God gave you those three babies for a reason, and He is NOT going to take you from them!" He said it so matter-of-factly that I had no choice but to simply trust him and believe him. I looked at him with tears in my eyes and said, "Okay, Dad."

The rest of the world must not have gotten the memo that I would be just fine though, because the next day, five different specialists with the hospital came into my prison cell with their teams traveling behind them to introduce themselves to me.

The first, of course, was the neurosurgeon and his team. He asked me a million questions about myself, and then asked about my babies at home. Then they left the room.

Next were a hematologist and his team. They asked a ton of questions and then said that they were going to take a whole bunch of my blood to have a look-see. Then they left the room.

Next came one of the doctors from my gastroenterologists' office. He sat on the side of my bed and also asked a lot of questions. Then he looked right in my eyes and said, "I heard how you were treated before coming to see us at our office. That doctor should have never treated you that way. That should have NEVER happened. I want you to know that I am going to take care of you!" Then he left the room.

Then a surgeon came in to talk to me about the rashes on my arms and how he was planning to do a biopsy. He spoke to me briefly–then he–you guessed it, left the room.

There was also a cardiologist who was looking after me. He came and described all sorts of pleasant tests that he wanted done.

I would also have to have a monitor hooked up to my chest by some young whippersnapper.

Lastly, there was the infectious disease specialist. He stood by my bed and asked questions also. However, he did something no one else had done. After looking at my arms at the rash that was there, he held on to my wrist and leaned in really close towards my face. For one horrible second, I thought he was going to kiss me! But after a brief moment he stood back up straight and patted my hand and said, "I am going to take care of you!" Then he left the room.

All throughout the day, family and friends had come to see me. They were all worried, and were coming out of the woodwork to be there. That made me worry more than anything that they all knew something that I didn't! Each time one of the specialists had come in to talk to me, there seemed to always be someone there that was able to help me explain to the next person what that particular doctor had said. Finally someone went to the gift shop to get me a notebook so that I could keep track of what was being said and done.

When that last specialist had come in, Dave was there. He had asked friends of ours to watch the babies so that he could come spend a couple of hours with me. This last doctor had us both perplexed though. After he had leaned in towards me and I thought he was going to kiss me, I looked at Dave and we exchanged glances. However, when the doctor left, it dawned on me what had just happened. I told Dave, "For a moment there, I thought he was going to kiss me!"

Dave and I both giggled a little over that, but then I said, "But he actually prayed over me, didn't he?"

"Yes," Dave said, "I believe he did!"

"Do you realize he's the second doctor to look at me and say 'I'm going to take care of you'?" I asked Dave.

We talked about how maybe God was speaking through them to let me know I would be ok! That God was going to take care of me, and He was telling me that through these men, both of whom seemed to have faith in God.

I stayed in the hospital for about a week, having about every test done that one could imagine. I was turned upside down and right side up. I was cut open and carved out of. I was poked and prodded until my arms looked like two over-bruised bananas! The hematologist actually found bacteria in my blood cells at one point, which indicated that I was septic. I was falling apart fast, yet no one was sure what the problem was, or if it was indeed only one problem, or coincidentally several problems surfacing all at once! The neurosurgeon said that the brain mass could either indicate multiple sclerosis, or a stroke. He wasn't sure, and said that even if he wanted to operate, which he couldn't because my blood wasn't clotting properly and I would bleed to death, it was in such a place that surgery could very well paralyze me. The cardiologist said that except for a murmur and irregular blood flow, he didn't see anything that would cause my illness, and believed that it was all due to whacky hormones! The biopsy that was taken from the rash on my upper body and arms didn't really show much of anything. The infectious disease specialist found nothing. The gastro doctor was the only one that gave me any sort of definite answer. He told me that the purple bruise-looking "rash" on my shins was some-thing called Arathyma Nodeosium. In his words, it was basically "the Crohn's disease manifesting itself in the skin." He explained that sometimes after a pregnancy the disease just goes "haywire" and that, more than likely, was what was happening with me. He said that between the pregnancy, a pregnancy with triplets none-theless, and then all of the stress I was under, my body went nuts!

Finally, one of the hematologist technicians came to my room and said this: "Well, we tested your blood again a couple of times, and although we had originally found bacteria in it, it's no longer there." Then she paused and said, "You came in here so broken, and now it's as though you're just fixed, and we didn't even really do anything!"

I explained to her that many people were praying for me, and that God had more He wanted from me. She asked if there was anything else she could do for me. At the same time, she and I both said, "Pray!"

FAITH WALK

* **Read Acts 16:16-40**

As I contemplated the "Faith Walk" for this chapter, I looked in one of my husband's Bibles, under the word "trust", in an index. That search led me to Acts 16. I continue to be amazed at how God works! He led me right to a scripture about Paul and Silas in prison.

Have you ever been in jail or prison? Sometimes, like me, even being in the hospital can feel like prison. From time to time, our home, marriage or career can feel like a prison. We've all felt stuck at some point in our lives.

I can't emphasize enough how God can take that situation and turn it around.

When my brother had his first brain surgery, there was a particular song he wanted to listen to while in the hospital. His wife bought him the CD so that he could have it right there with him. It was another time Kathy Tracollis' music played a part in our lives, as it was a song of hers.

During this time in the hospital, I wrote those same words out and posted them on the bulletin board in my hospital room right next to a picture of my babies. The words are the chorus from her song, "The Twenty-Third Psalm".

> *"Lord, heal me! Please free me. I know You hear my prayer.*
> *Lord, love me! Please touch me. I need You here."*

Just like Paul and Silas, I tried my best to *sing* in my prison cell. When you find yourself in a prison, no matter what kind it is, sing. Then wait for the Lord.

Chapter 23

HEALING

AFTER A WEEKS' STAY, I was released from the hospital, with instructions to come back for another MRI and an appointment with the neurosurgeon on May 29th. It felt like a long way away to me, since it was now the middle of April, but I figured they wanted to give me some time to let my body keep healing.

Little by little my body did heal, and I started to feel better every day. When my birthday finally came around on April 29th, I felt so good that I met a friend of mine for lunch! In the meantime I had my second MRI and was just waiting to go back to the doctor in May.

On my way home from lunch, however, Dave called to tell me that the doctor's office had called and said I missed my appointment. I told him, "No, they are mistaken, because my card from the hospital says May 29th."

He told me that he told them that too, but they said that it was supposed to be Monday, April 29th, and that the hospital wrote it down wrong. He told them that I was actually out their direction and could come in ASAP, but they said that I would have to wait until Friday at this point. I got off the phone with Dave and called them. I told them that this was my brain we were talking about and that I couldn't wait until Friday. I asked if there wasn't any way he could just tell me, even over the phone, what he thought it was that they were seeing on the MRI. The nurse said she would talk to the doctor and get back to me.

In the meantime, I was driving right by his office so I just pulled in. All I could think about was the fact that there was something in my brain that shouldn't be there, and now that I knew they had possibly gotten some answers, it was going to drive me crazy waiting for another day, let alone almost a week, to find out! I parked and marched right up to his office and told the nurse, "I know it's the end of the day, and that you said you would call me back, but I have to know."

Then, before I could go on, she said, "I was just going to call you back. He can see you; come on," and she led me into his office.

He sat there at his desk and offered me the seat on the other side. He never stood up and hardly even looked up. He shuffled some papers around on top of the desk, then said to me without looking directly at me, "Well, I don't know what it was, but whatever was there is not anymore."

That's it! That's all he said, and so I sat there stunned! Before I could get any words to come out of my mouth, he finally looked me in the eyes and said, "That's a GOOD thing!"

Through the tears in my eyes, I said, "Yes, yes it is."

He told me that he wanted me to follow up with a neurologist, and that the neurologist would probably order another MRI, but that he didn't see any reason for me to keep seeing him. I thanked him and practically ran to the van!

I called Dave and told him that it was GONE! We rejoiced and cried over the phone together and praised God! We knew that I had just been healed!

After that, I called my mom and dad. Mom answered and through my tears I exclaimed, "There's nothing there! It's gone! My brain! There's nothing there!"

Stunned and confused, my mom thought I was my sister who was going through a very nasty divorce at the time, and thought she had finally completely lost her mind! After I explained that it was me, not my sister, and that the tumor was gone, she also rejoiced with me, and we laughed and cried!

That day I told everyone that I ran into! I told family and friends. I told strangers at the store and the teller at the bank! I swore from that day on that I would tell people everywhere what God had just done. I promised Him that I would tell anyone that would listen that we serve a God who still heals today! What a wonderful birthday it turned out to be!

I had literally been knocked down, physically beaten. But by God's hand and grace, I was able to Get Up and Walk. I was wheeled into the hospital on one night, and a week later I got up and walked out! I walked out healed!

FAITH WALK

"ţlîthā qūmi!"

No, I haven't "flipped my wig"—Talitha koum (the spelling in *The Message Bible* and most other contemporary versions of the Bible) is what Jesus once said—in Aramaic—to a little girl. It means, "Little girl, get up!"

   * ***Read Mark 5:21-43***

* *In these verses, Jesus healed two different people. Who were they?*

* *What reasons does the Bible give for Jesus healing these two people?*

* *How were each of them healed?*

Whether it's a physical illness or an emotional stress that's plaguing you, Jesus wants to heal you. If it's your marriage or relationship(s), He wants to heal you. Maybe it's your past that keeps popping up to threaten your present, and your future; well, He can heal that too!

God sometimes allows us to be healed through doctors and modern medicine! Have you or someone you know experienced a healing like this?

Sometimes our body just fights things off, because God created them to do so!

Sometimes, God doesn't allow our bodies to be healed, but allows our minds to be healed so that we are able to cope with "the thorn in our flesh." 2 Corinthians 12:9-10 (*The Message*) says, "He said to me; 'My grace is enough; it's all you need. My strength comes into its own in your weakness.' Once I heard that, I was glad to let it happen. I quit focusing on the handicap and began appreciating the gift. It was a case of Christ's strength moving in on my weakness. Now I take limitations in stride, and with good cheer, these limitations that cut me down to size—abuse, accidents, opposition, bad breaks. I just let Christ take over! And so the weaker I get, the stronger I become."

Although God healed me of the tumor, I still have Crohn's Disease. However, I believe that God uses my illness every day for His glory.

Then there are times God does a miraculous thing, and He supernaturally heals!

However, the greatest healing we will ever experience, is the one that will occur for those of us who have asked Christ into our lives. We will receive the *ultimate healing* someday when we get to Heaven, where there is no more death or crying or pain (Revelation 21:4).

Chapter 24

FROM THE "FRYING PAN INTO THE FIRE?"

SHORTLY AFTER I WAS RELEASED from the hospital, we were called for an interview at a church not far from where my parents lived. We were excited to maybe be able to minister in a church so close to home. If we got the church, we could go home for Sunday dinner each week! We made so many plans before even interviewing.

The interview went well, and we really liked the people. When they voted on whether or not to offer Dave the position as their pastor, it was unanimous! They called to let us know, and we accepted! The only thing left to do was decide on a move-in date, and pack up our belongings and go!.

However, after a few days, Dave talked to a gentleman from the board of the church. As they were discussing the reasons we left the church in Michigan—because of black mold—this member told Dave that they had had some flooding in this parsonage as well. He explained to Dave that he didn't believe there was any black mold there.

After Dave told me about the conversation, we both had the same thought. We weren't sure we wanted to take our family to another home that could possibly be the same, if not worse, than what we had picked up our entire lives and moved from! The pastor and wife that were leaving this church were still living in the parsonage, so Dave called to talk to them.

They were relieved that he did, because they said they didn't want to stand in the way of God's will, but since we were inquiring, they felt that we should know that the basement had had a flooding problem in the past. They said they didn't want to sway our decision, so suggested that Dave come and take a look at the basement with a more critical eye than maybe the first time through.

Dave went over to take a look, and when he came home, told me that there were spots in the basement that looked worse than what we had ran from! He said that as they talked about it, it came out that the basement had flooded so badly in the past that there had been raw sewage in it! The pastoral couple living there said that we needed to do what we felt led to do, but that they really didn't think it was a good idea to bring babies into this house either.

So, needless to say, Dave called our District Superintendent and explained why we would have to not take the church. This was a hard thing for us to do, because this was our first interview within the Wesleyan denomination. We thought for sure that after turning down the church after being voted in and accepting it, we would not be offered anything else. We were pleasantly surprised.

FAITH WALK

* *Read 1 Kings 3:1-15*

* *What did King Solomon ask God for?*

* *Why did God give Solomon what he asked for?*

* *Have you ever made a really bad decision? What were the consequences?*

We were right on the verge of making a bad decision because we were paying more attention to our desire to be near family. God intervened at the last moment—He probably figured we had already been through too much—and He stopped us from making a poor choice.

"Lord, grand us wisdom as you did King Solomon. Help us to always desire to make good choices for ourselves and our families. Guide us into good judgment and understanding in the situations in which we find ourselves . Lead us every step of the way, enabling us to have fewer regrets and more peace in our decisions."

Chapter 25

HOME

NOT EVEN A WEEK WENT by before we received another call from the Wesleyan District Superintendent, Dr. Jeff Mansell. During the entire time we started looking for something with the Wesleyan Church in Ohio, we had our eyes on this one particular church. It was back up near the hospital where we had had the babies, and still not too far away from my family. It seemed like a nice area, and a nice church, so we kept talking about how nice it would be to get an interview there, but that we probably wouldn't, because that's "just how things go for us."

The call that we received after turning the other church down was for the very church that we had dreamed of! Dave came running up the stairs of our rental house that day, and said to me, "You will never guess what he just said!" He panted, "He said that he understands completely and has another church that he thinks would fit us perfectly... It's the church we have been looking at!"

We jumped around and danced right in the middle of the living room! We were so excited!

Dave called the church contact person, and set up a phone

interview with the board. Soon after that, they called us for an actual face-to-face interview in which we would both sit in on and talk with the board. The interview would be on a Saturday, and then Dave would preach and I would sing on Sunday.

Everything went so well, and when they called to tell us that they had voted unanimously to call us to their church, we had no doubt that it was the place God had for us.

Almost one full year after leaving our last church and moving completely on faith, we packed up to move to our new home.

The day we moved, we had planned on arriving at our new home by five pm. Five turned into eight and eight turned into eleven. The moving truck that Dave and a friend of ours were driving refused to go over fifty-five miles per hour. At one point along the route, Dave told me to go on ahead in the van with the babies and get them somewhat settled.

When I arrived, worn out with cranky babies in tow, I barely made it out of the van before our new church family started to grab babies and hug me. We got the babies fed and then sat around in a circle of lawn chairs and waited for the men to arrive with all of our worldly possessions.

When eleven o'clock rolled around and they pulled into the parking lot, Dave said he cried. You see, the last time we moved to a church, the only ones helping us move were two of my brothers and a friend of ours! Even though there were a few people from the church there, they wanted to talk more than move. He said he was so tired and worn out from the moving and then the drive, that when he saw TWENTY people from this new church sitting there, waiting to help, he lost it and cried like a baby!

We started the move-in process and I was soon delegated as the person to sit in the garage and tell everyone where to put things. I liked that job immensely!

The next morning was Sunday, and we were to have our installation service with the District Superintendent leading the morning worship. Wow, we were so tired. Not only had we had a horribly long night from moving, but also we had three babies who didn't sleep well!

The service was beautiful, though, and we got to meet everyone and were welcomed thoroughly. At one point, we had a greeting time, and as I walked around and shook hands with our new family, an older man came up to me and took my hand and simply said, "Welcome Home."

That's all he said. Welcome Home. It hit me in that moment that I finally was where I belonged after such a long, rough year of not knowing what was coming next or if we would ever find a home! When Pastor Jeff (the District Superintendent) called us up along with our babies in order to "install" us, and welcome us to the church and the district, I cried. I didn't think the tears would ever stop.

It was a combination of emotions that just came welling up within me and started to spill over all at once, and I didn't see an end in sight! I thought of all that we had been through, and all that we now had to look forward to. I felt loved and safe and cared for. They were feelings of knowing I was exactly where I was supposed to be, exactly when I was supposed to be. They were the emotions of a new mom welling up and spilling out. It was the knowledge of a new, safe home in which to abide! It was a realization that God had healed me for a purpose, and part of that purpose was this very moment in this very place. It was thankfulness for family, and life, and my husband and children. It was an overwhelming sense of Home! Finally, we were home. And so there was nothing left for me to do but cry. Looking back, they probably thought they had a basket case on their hands and wondered, "What in the world did we do by bringing her here?" However, no one said a word ; they just let me cry and they hugged me and welcomed me and loved me from that day on. For at that very moment, I was home.

FAITH WALK

* ***Read 2 Corinthians 1:3-4***

In *The Message Bible*, this section of scripture is entitled The Rescue.

> *"All praise to the God and Father of our Master, Jesus the Messiah! Father of all mercy! God of all healing counsel! He comes alongside us when we go through hard times, and before you know it, he brings us alongside someone else who is going through hard times so that we can be there for that person just as God was there for us."*

I don't know about you, but that's comforting to me. Not only will He be there for us, He gives us each other so that we can help hold one another up in the hard times.

* ***What does home mean to you?***

* ***Do you have a church that you can call home?***

Everywhere we go on this earth we are going to find people that hurt us, let us down or act like hypocrites. Nowhere in the Bible does it say we must have several church services a week in order to be good Christians. As I said a few chapters back, we don't have to even be *within* church walls to ask Jesus to be part of our lives. Still, it is important to have that fellowship, and to find a church to attend where you can learn and grow in your faith. The Bible does say in Hebrews 10:24-25, "Let's see how inventive we can be in encouraging love and helping out, not avoiding worshiping together as some do but spurring each other on, especially as we see the big Day approaching." (Message) The "big Day" that this passage refers to is the Day that Jesus Christ will come to claim those who believe in Him.

Church should be a safe place, separate from the world, but embracing the world. A place where we can be the same person we are the rest of the week, and be accepted and loved. A place where we learn, worship and grow in our faith without fear of rejection. Dave constantly tells our congregation, "People get beat up enough out there in the real world. Church should be a place where they can come and feel safe."

If your church isn't providing that safe, loving environment to others, change it!

Chapter 26

SMALL TOWN PROMISED LAND

HOME. HOME SOON BECAME CHAOTIC, as we tried to adjust to our new surroundings. The babies especially had a hard time sleeping through the night, just because it was a new place, and they were only fifteen months old! They were just getting to the point of being used to the house we were in, and then POOF, they were in a new one again.

Dave and I were also overwhelmed because we now had this big house to organize! However, after a week to get settled in, my parents came to help. I don't know how we ever would have gotten along without their love and support over the years. One day, Mom and I took a break and I told her I wanted to show her something. Up until this day, she had only seen our new home and church, and the road that got Dad and her here!

We drove downtown to the store to pick something up, and then I asked her to take a little walk with me. I wanted to show her something I had just discovered. Our new town was right along the Maumee River in the picturesque village of Grand Rapids, Ohio. A quiet little town, there's an old-fashioned candy store with the candy jars like I used to see in "The Little House on The Prairie" TV show. At the time, there were only a couple of restaurants and a pizza shop, but no McDonald's or other "fast food" for at least 20 miles. Instead of hotels, we had bed and breakfasts. So I took Mom down to show her a bit of the town, and then we took a little walk.

I took her behind all the stores to what's called the towpath, and showed her the river. The towpath in Grand Rapids is a beautiful site. There are stationary swings placed along it that an entire family could sit on and watch the river, or where a couple out for a romantic walk at sunset could simply sit and hold hands.

At this moment though, it was just Mom and I overlooking the river. We didn't take the time right then to sit on a swing; we just stood there. For a moment we were silently taking in the beauty, and then I felt tears in my eyes. I felt a calm come over me, and knew without any doubt in my mind, for the first time in my life, that I was exactly where God wanted me to be.

I told her, "I feel like for the last year we have been wandering in the desert, and we've finally come to our Promised Land. This, right here, is what God had in mind for us all along.

"This beautiful little village is the place that God already had planned back when we found out we were having triplets and I told Dave, 'We can't do this. We don't have the home or the finances for this, but God has something in mind for us.'

"This is the place, and the home, and the church family that He had planned all along! I know it with everything in my heart," I told mom.

We soon became settled in our new home and started to enjoy the neighborhood a little more. It was a huge culture shock to us both, having come from larger cities.

Where I grew up in Akron, Ohio, we lived in a nice, quiet little neighborhood. However, on every side of us, only fifteen minutes away, was a mall or major city, and "fast food" was something we could easily get to from our home if we wanted to! We had shopping centers close by, and major grocery stores were where we easily did our grocery shopping. Dave grew up in Cuyahoga Falls, Ohio, and was used to a lot of "busyness" everywhere around him, as they lived close to an expressway.

He, of course, had lived other places since then, and when we married, we lived in a duplex off of a major expressway. Within walking distance, there were many stores and restaurants.

So, walking around our home in the village of Grand Rapids gave to me a feeling of being on a campground like we would go to when I was a child, and saying hi to everyone you saw. In fact, state and privately owned campgrounds were on all sides of us! I was now living where other people vacationed, and for good reason. It was beautiful!

One of the first walks with the babies I had taken let me know that "I was not in Kansas anymore, Toto." We were passing a woman that was also out for a walk. She said "Hi" and stopped to ask about the babies. When she noticed that they were triplets, she exclaimed, "Oh, you must be the new pastor's wife at the Wesleyan church!"

I was excited! I thought to myself, "*Awesome! Here's one of our parishioners and she lives right in my neighborhood!*"

I told her, "Yes, I am!" introduced the babies, and said, "So, you must go to the church?"

"Oh no," she said, "I just heard about you."

That was my first true taste of small town living, as I soon came to realize that here, everyone knows everyone or is related to everyone, or knows someone who is related to someone who knows someone's uncle! Any way you slice it, pretty much everyone knows everyone's business. I told Dave that could be a good thing! Unless it's a bad thing!

The ladies planned a dinner outing not long after we were settled in, while my mom was still here. We had such a nice time, but even though the restaurant that we went to was about a half hour away, the ladies from the church still ran into several people that they knew. I would later come to have a couple of good friends that told me, "When you first came here you asked us if there was anyone we didn't know, but now everywhere we go it's *you* that runs into someone you know!"

So, yes, it took a while, but I adapted quickly and smoothly to small town life and have loved every minute of it!

FAITH WALK

* ***Read Joshua 1***

Can you imagine how the Israelites must have felt when they were finally able to reach their promised land after forty years of wandering in the desert?

After all that time—after Moses had passed away—Joshua woke up one morning and God told him to "Get going. Cross this Jordan River, you and all the people. Cross to the country I'm giving to the People of Israel."

Finally, it was time to go home. Time to claim the land God had promised to them.

It was their own fault that they hadn't received it sooner. They whined and cried and complained, instead of doing the things they were told.

* *Can you think of a time when you knew you were exactly where God wanted you to be?*

Sometimes we get in our own way. If we would just step aside and let God take the lead, we would be so much better off.

Chapter 27

AN EASTER
DEDICATION

WHEN THE BABIES TURNED TWO, we had a big party and invited everyone from church and of course my family to come. We had an inflatable pool out for all the little ones, a sprinkler, and lots of food, fun and fellowship.

With all of the moving that we had to do when they were first born, we had never had the babies dedicated. In the Wesleyan Church, to have your child(ren) "dedicated" is to take them in front of your family and church family and publicly say, "These children belong to God, and are a gift from Him to us. We are promising today to raise them in the ways of the Holy Bible, and teach them about Jesus and His love." Then the pastor will ask the family and the church family if they will assist the parents in support and prayer in raising their child or children in the ways of God. It's basically a time to thank God for the children He's given and dedicate them back to Him!

There were no "church laws" saying that we couldn't have

them dedicated, even though we were moving around a lot at first. Dave brought it up once to me and others asked us about doing it. However, Dave and I did dedicate them in our hearts to God. God knew that we were thankful and that we dedicated them to Him. Still we didn't want to do a public dedication until we were with a church family that would love our babies and who deserved to be a part of their lives.

I didn't want to jump in and do it, just because everyone expected it. I knew that no matter where we ended up when it did happen, that our family would come for it, and so I wanted to wait and see.

Needless to say, knowing that we had finally found the place that we were meant to be, we were ready to plan that dedication. We asked my uncle, who is a pastor and lives only about forty-five minutes from us, to come and do the service. Then we planned a time. Easter is my favorite holiday, not because of candy and bunnies, but because of what it symbolizes.

It's the holiday that we celebrate the day that Jesus conquered death and rose from the grave. We celebrate on that day that we have eternal life if we believe in Him! On Easter we are reminded that everything that is of Jesus, is made new!

It's the time of year when birds start singing again, flowers start blooming, and pieces of grass can be seen popping up. It reminds me of hope! So, I asked Dave if we could have their dedication on Easter Sunday, because I couldn't think of a more special time to present my children to the Lord in thanks! Easter is when "God so loved the world, that He gave His only begotten Son, that whoever believes in Him should not perish, but have everlasting life!" (John 3:16, NKJV)

"Hey, Jesus! Where You Goin'?"

This picture was taken on Easter Dedication Sunday, 2003

FAITH WALK

* ***Read Luke 23, 24***

There is no other religion in the world that can claim, nor do they claim, that their 'god' is able to have a personal relationship with his followers.

God, the God of Christianity, sent His Son Jesus, so that we could have a personal relationship with Him. It's easy for people to say, "Whatever you want to believe is fine; we all have to believe something."

I guarantee you that the I Am is the only God who offers to live in you, and I can bear witness to the fact that He truly does. I've lived without Him, and I've lived with Him. The years with Him, have been the best by far. I truly would not be here otherwise.

Chapter 28

JUICE

OVER THE FIRST SEVERAL YEARS in our new home and church, I had to have some blood transfusions. The first one was the scariest. I worried about AIDS and other diseases. I knew that people sometimes had to have blood transfusions and that it was a GREAT thing! I knew it saved lives! But when it came time for me to have one, all I could think of was that some stranger's blood would be coursing through MY veins! I cried in the doctor's office the day she told me that my blood level was too low, and that I needed to seriously consider a transfusion and let her know within just a couple of days. I went home and prayed about it, and cried over it and worried over it, and then I let it go! God had worked so many things out for me so far; how could I not trust Him in this? So the next day, I called the doctor and let her know that I would do the transfusion.

My mom and dad happened to be visiting again at that time, so Dad went with me. I think he was as nervous as I, remembering what he had seen me go through the last time we were at a hospital together. He has said several times since then that he has "never seen anyone so sick, and with so many things wrong all at once", as when I was in the hospital. However, I had a peace, and although my human side kept trying to worry, the Holy Spirit within me kept settling my heart.

As God would have it, everything worked out fine, and I felt like a new woman! I had not realized having enough blood in your body could make you feel so good! Friends would look at me and say, "You have color in your cheeks again!" Or they would tell me, "You glow!"

You would think by those comments that I had just gotten married, instead of getting some "juice"' as we have ended up calling it.

Several times over the years, I have had to get "juice," and every time I do, I feel like a new woman. So, you see, God may supernaturally heal us, or He may use these doctors and researchers that He has spent so much time giving knowledge to, in order to heal us.

Don't get me wrong, there have been times when a doctor has wanted me to take a certain medication that I didn't feel right about for some reason. The only thing I could attribute it to at the time was God letting me know that the particular drug or procedure was not what would be best, so I turned it down.

Unfortunately, there were a couple of times I didn't turn away a treatment, and I should have. I once decided to try a doctor who was into natural therapies. When that didn't work, he gave me an immunosuppressant drug that put me in the hospital. It wore down my immune system too much, and when I became ill, I became septic—again—and spent a couple of days in the hospital.

It had been several years since my first hospitalization and I was seeing a new doctor up near our new home. For some reason, this particular office kept making my appointments with the nurse practitioner instead of a doctor. I have no problem seeing a nurse practitioner at all, but she was all I *ever* saw. She mentioned putting me on a drug called Remicade, which I didn't mind trying, but the other thing she wanted me to take along with it was another drug called Immuran. I told her about the experience I'd had in 2002 and that I didn't feel comfortable taking it. She spoke to one of the doctors in the office—it was never the same one—and they agreed to try the Remicade without the other drug.

Unfortunately, over time we realized that I wasn't making much progress on the Remicade alone. She explained to me that one of the doctors said that it was most likely the pregnancy that had put me in the hospital, not the Immuran. She wore me down, and I agreed to take the medication.

Less than forty-eight hours after my first dose, I was sick and passing out. Dave had to call 911 in the middle of the night for me to be taken to the hospital. I was in tachycardia when I arrived, and later found out I was also once again septic. Once the medicine was out of my system, I was well and able to go home again. For the third time in ten years, I was near death with sepsis. Moreover, for the third time, I left the hospital completely well and whole.

As the nurse waited with me for Dave to get the car, she said to me and our visiting friend that she didn't understand how I was leaving so soon. It had only been two days since I came into the hospital extremely sick and septic. She wondered how I could be well and going home now. I explained to her that this was actually not the first time I had been this ill and that God always pulled me out of it. I know now that there are certain medications that I have to stay away from. I have faith that God will always guide me in what to do in every other aspect of my life, so why would He stop guiding me when it comes to medical advice? He wouldn't.

I trust the doctors and nurses to give great advice, and then

I trust God to let me know what advice to take and what advice to leave. So far, I'm still kickin', so He must be working through medications! I just have to listen to Him!

FAITH WALK

* ***Do you know that Luke, one of the apostles and an author of the Bible, was a doctor?***

You could probably understand how I might be "anti-doctor" after reading some of the difficulties I've had with some of them. However, I am thankful that God has given us, as lowly humans, the knowledge we need in order for doctors to exist! Without doctors, we would all be sick and dropping like flies.

Do not be afraid to ask to "interview" a new doctor before letting him or her treat you. This is someone you are putting into a powerful place when it comes to your body. You have the right to make an appointment to talk with this person and see if he or she is someone you feel like you could trust.

Ask God to guide you to the right doctors and then pray for them.

Chapter 29

WHO, ME?

AFTER A WHILE, EVERYTHING WAS going so well that I almost forgot that I had a disease! Before having the babies, I was one big, constant mess. It seemed as though the flare-ups with the Crohn's Disease were constant. However, after having that time in the hospital when everything just went crazy, the disease seemed to subside for a while.

Then one day I began to feel worn down, so I went to the doctor. As we sat there and talked, she asked me how I felt about anti-depressants. This was a new doctor so I reminded her that I actually took some, but I was put on those years ago only because of some problems with headaches I used to have, and that it was not because I was depressed.

She explained to me that we don't have to hate life and feel suicidal to be depressed. She pointed out to me that even the strongest of people would need some help after all that I had been through.

I didn't disagree with her, but explained that I was happy to be in such a "good place" in life now, and that if I had been depressed through it all, it would surely not be now!

Then she also pointed out a list of things that are major stressors:

- Death in the family
- Having a child
- Moving
- Financial stress
- Major illness

"Julie," she gently said, "you have had ALL of these things, some of them multiple times, in an extremely short period of time. Within one year to be exact, and most people only have maybe one of these within a year."

She then suggested that we just "up" the anti-depressant I had been taking and see what happened. "Just try it and see if it doesn't help you, ok?" she asked.

I did, and you know what? It did make a difference, a huge difference. You see, I found out that in our family, a chemical imbalance resides. It's nothing major, and it's not to the point that illnesses such as Bipolar Disorder or other mental illnesses exist, but depression certainly does! It was all starting to make sense to me as to why I felt certain ways growing up and through life!

I only wish we had realized it sooner; it would have saved a lot of heartache. Not only in my immediate family, but extended family also.

I want to take the time to say here that my immediate family growing up had a good and happy home, free of alcohol, drugs, smoking or anything like that. It was a good Christian home, and most all of our extended family is Christian, with lots of pastors within to show it!

However, being a Christian family does not necessarily make you exempt from human faults. Our bodies are subjects of a fallen world and are not immune to sin, sickness and disease. If God meant every Christian to immediately be healed through faith, then it would not say in the Bible, "He will wipe every tear from their eyes. There will be no more death or mourning or crying or pain, for the old order of things has passed away." Revelation 21:4

God can, as I know, heal us. He can, and He does, take away sickness. However, sometimes, He lets something stay with us, in order for us to help someone else, to be humbled, or maybe even because of sinful behavior. The only thing that I can tell you that He will FOR SURE do if we ask is forgive us our sins, and send His Holy Spirit to live within us. The rest is up to Him to decide. So if we ask, and our prayers are not answered the way that we think they should be or want them to be, don't ever think that God has "left you." Don't ever let someone tell you, "You just don't have enough faith!" In addition, never, EVER doubt God and His infinite wisdom. He cares for us more than we care for ourselves, and He knows what is best for us in the end.

Therefore, when someone asks me, "Why did He heal you of 'this thing' but not from 'that thing'?", I tell him or her, because He's God and He knows what's best for me, and I choose to trust that.

God backed up my trust through this doctor's appointment discussing depression. Back when the neurosurgeon told me that "Whatever was there is no longer there," there were people that said things like:

"Maybe it was just a spot on the film, and there was nothing there in the first place?"

Or, "If you moved at all during the MRI, then it could have made it look like something was there."

The funny thing is that these two quotes came from two entirely different people, but people that should have believed either in the accuracy of the equipment, or in the supremacy of God and His ability to heal!

You see, one was the neurologist that the surgeon had sent me to for a follow up. He saw the films himself and you would think that he would know the difference between a "spot from move-ment" and a "potential brain tumor."

The other was a Christian and a fellow pastor's wife. Instead of believing that God healed me, she chose to believe that nothing was there in the first place.

Again, I was choosing to trust. I chose to believe that God had healed me. It was because of that trust that God chose to show them that it was indeed He that healed me, and not some "fluke."

The next MRI that I had done through the neurologist showed that the mass was still gone, but this time, in its place was scar tissue! Yes, God has a sense of humor! He decided to show them in a way no one would have ever thought of. By placing scar tissue where the tumor had been without my ever having surgery to remove it, He proved to them that it was in fact the Great Physician that took care of this one!

When I saw my current doctor for the headaches I was hav-ing along with being worn out, she ordered another MRI because of my history. I told her I had had several over the last couple of years, and everything was fine, but she simply wanted to make sure. Therefore, two years after first being told I had a brain mass, I was back to the MRI. Again, the report came back that only scar tissue remained, and that everything else looked fine.

It has been about ten years since I was healed. I no longer see a neurologist, and I no longer worry about it coming back.

At the writing of this book, 2010, my last MRI was approxi-mately two years ago, due once again to some headaches. The doctor I now see has records from my past, but knows nothing of the brain tumor or how sick I had once been. So, when the report came back, she flippantly read off that there was a "normal brain," and moved on to sinuses as the cause of my headaches.

I stopped her and said, "Could you tell me again what the MRI report said?"

She looked at me rather strangely, but repeated the report for me.

I became teary eyed and thanked her. When she looked at me like I had gone mad, I said to her, "You don't understand, but to me that report is amazing!"

I then explained everything. After she listened to the whole story, she looked at me with much compassion and said, "Would you like to have a copy of this?"

I told her I would, and I left the office that day with the best reminder in the world of God's love for me!

FAITH WALK

* ***Read Psalm 143***

David, the Psalmist, got depressed. A lot.

Quite a few of the Psalms show David's depression, and yet, Jesus Himself came from the line of David, so did depression make David any less "holy?"

As I have mentioned previously, God heals us in different ways. One of those ways is sometimes through medication. There are many who will tell you, "You don't need medication; you only need Jesus."

While I agree that I could make it on Jesus alone, I'm here to tell you that I wouldn't always be the best human being I could be while I was "making it."

Medications for depression are a touchy subject among many Christians, but sometimes it's not a soul problem. Sometimes it is simply a result of faulty wiring, or the hazards of life wearing on our bodies.

God and I? We're good! I assure you of that. He lives in me and through me and we have an awesome relationship! I also happen to know that He's ok with me taking an anti-depressant. If you think you may be depressed, sure—pray about it—but do not feel like you're not being a good Christian if you need to take a medication. And don't ever stop taking your medication without talking to your physician first.

Chapter 30

GET UP AND WALK

I HAD JUST STARTED WRITING this book when I found myself sitting at an empty information desk at the Cleveland Clinic in Cleveland, Ohio.

It was a little after seven P.M. and I had been there since seven-thirty A.M. My baby brother had had his second brain surgery in ten years, and although he was supposed to be in recovery waking up, he was taken back to surgery because of bleeding in his brain. It was supposed to only take an hour, but we found ourselves waiting that hour, and then another hour. The waiting was so hard.

My husband and kids were at home, and I was there with my sister-in-law and the kids, my mom and dad. We were in a small waiting room full of our family and another family just as big as ours. It felt like there were about 100 restless children in "our" waiting room, and we were all feeling anxious, worried, tired, and yes, cranky... Some of you probably know those feelings.

While all the "grown–ups" were trying not to worry, the kids from both families in the waiting room became fast friends and all started to play LOUDLY together. Kids just don't get it. They do not have the worries that adults have. Sitting at that little desk taking it all in, I was reminded of Matthew 6:27. "Who of you by worrying can add a single hour to his life?" OUCH!

There I was—even though I had personally seen God do miraculous things for my family over the last ten years, and knew that He had taken such good care of us—still worrying.

I am sure God was there, watching over our little waiting room as it was getting smaller by the minute. Shaking His head, I'm sure He was probably saying, "Julie, Julie, Julie, why in the world, after all you and I have gone through together, after all that I've helped you through, after the struggles you and your family have faced yet made it through—why are you still worrying?"

Some of you may have had a loved one in the hospital and worried about them all day, or maybe even got horrible news and weren't able to take them home with you. It could have been your baby, your parent, or your spouse. Maybe a friend or some other loved one. On the other hand, maybe you had wonderful news at the end of that day, week, month, year, or even years! And you all lived "Happily Ever After."

We wondered that night at the Cleveland Clinic if we would get our "Happily Ever After". We had thought so. We were all very hopeful because of how well he had done 10 years ago when he first had brain surgery, and the waiting room started to feel like any other family gathering. However, earlier that morning when they called my sister-in-law to talk to the doctor, she came back in tears. She said that they had had a hard time waking Jamie, my brother, up, and as they took out the breathing tube, he seized. The surgery was supposed to take care of those seizures, so they did a CAT scan to check things out. They found that there was a pool of blood where they had removed the tumor, and we were told they would be taking him back into surgery.

For a while, we all sat and looked at each other and silently prayed. We were numb. I couldn't take it anymore, so I left the room and found a place to get on my laptop. Then the doctor came in to talk with us, and said that although Jamie wasn't awake yet, he was in recovery and they were able to stop the bleeding. She told us that his left side would be paralyzed, but that they were hopeful that he would regain feeling on that side over time.

Since it had ended up being so late, and I had already talked to Dave and the kids to say goodnight, I planned to go ahead and stay at Mom and Dad's for the night and head home in the morning. Against my mom's "motherly concern", I decided to drive the forty-five minutes back to their house by myself.

"No, Mom," I said, "I don't need anyone to ride with me. I will see you at the house!"

After we walked the maze that is the Cleveland Clinic, and finally found our cars again, we all headed to Hartville, Ohio, in the opposite direction of my husband and children. I called my husband to let him know how Jamie was doing and that although we were all feeling a little down about the outcome so far, we were all too tired to go on without some sleep, so we were heading "home" for the night.

Following that conversation I heard a loud "clinking" noise, and I was no longer able to control the steering wheel of my car well! I pulled off the highway and into a gas station. As I pulled the car in, I prayed quickly, "Lord, let me come across some nice guy who's a mechanic and is willing to help me out a little."

I parked cockeyed in a handicap spot because it was the first thing I came to, and called my husband back. As I was talking to Dave, I saw a man with a blue "mechanics" type shirt come out of the gas station store, so I yelled over to him, "Are you a mechanic by any chance?"

I was fully trusting that God would give me a mechanic! This man looked at me as if I had two heads and said "No!", and walked to his car in the opposite direction.

I knew then that I needed to call AAA, but I suppose I was hoping a mechanic would be able to quickly fix it, or at least tell me what was wrong.

I stood there again with my hood up this time, and out walked another man. I was too embarrassed from my last encounter with the "non-mechanic", so I kept my mouth shut and hoped that the popped up hood would speak for me. I also realized I must have been in a very bad part of town, because just in the ten minutes or so that I stood there, I saw several policemen pull in, go into the gas station's store, and leave again.

I carry protection of my choice, so I made sure I had it handy. When I noticed the next man come out, I just stood there.

He went to the car next to me, but then stopped and said to me, "Are you having a problem? I'm a mechanic; maybe I can help!"

I'm sure God was having Himself a good chuckle at this point! If I had just waited on *His* timing, I would have gotten my mechanic without making a spectacle of myself.

I answered that I was indeed having a problem. I explained all about the "clinking noise," so he looked and discovered that my serpentine belt was missing.

We spoke for a moment, and he cautioned me not to drive with it missing at all, but to call for roadside assistance. I thanked him, and he left. Then I thanked the Lord for sending my mechanic!

I called AAA and gave the woman a good laugh as I accidentally told her that my "serendipity belt" had fallen off on the highway! Then I went inside to tell the clerk at the gas station why I was randomly parked crooked in the handicap spot, and that I would soon be leaving with the assistance of a tow truck. After all, with all of the police cars pulling in and out, I certainly didn't want to be on *their* radar!

Surprisingly sooner rather than later, a person came with a tow truck and got me on the road. To my surprise, as we pulled out of the gas station, I saw that a police station was situated right across the street! It turned out the neighborhood probably was not so bad after all!

The next morning, my mom came to wake me earlier than we had planned. She said that they had received a call from my sister-in-law saying that the doctors were taking Jamie for another MRI soon, and some more tests.

The nurses were having a hard time waking him, and the new worry was that he had suffered a stroke.

Devastated, Mom, Dad and I made the forty-five-minute drive worried about what we would find at the hospital when we got there. What we found was not what we expected at all!

When we tracked down my two sisters-in-law, we were told that within the time that it took us to drive there, Jamie had started to wake up. They discovered that he had not had a stroke! Praise the Lord!

In the days to follow, little by little, Jamie began to move his left side. First his arm, then his leg, and when I was finally able to leave several days later, they were already talking about where he would go for rehabilitation.

I knew that God had allowed me to be stranded with my brother. If my car had not broken down and been out of commission for several days, I would have been torn between going home to my husband and babies, and staying with my baby brother. Within just a couple of weeks, Jamie was released from rehab to go home to his family in time for Christmas. He was able to Get Up...and Walk.

FAITH WALK

As I ponder a last scripture to give you, something to make God real to you, I'm not sure what to do. Two different scriptures have come to mind, so I'm going to give them to you straight, right here, right now. If you do not take away anything else from this book, take this:

John 14:11-14 (*The Message*) "Believe me: I am in my Father and my Father is in me. If you can't believe that, believe what you see—these works. The person who trusts me will not only do what I'm doing but even greater things, because I, on my way to the Father, am giving you the same work to do that I've been doing. You can count on it. From now on, whatever you request along the lines of who I am and what I am doing, I'll do it. That's how the Father will be seen for who he is in the Son. I mean it. Whatever you request in this way, I'll do."

The other one is this. Read John chapter 4, but I'm going to give you verse 42: "They said to the woman, 'We're no longer taking this on your say-so. We've heard it for ourselves and know it for sure. He's the Savior of the world!'"

Epilogue

I WANT TO REMIND YOU that God is still the God of miracles. God still heals brains. He still restores our bodies. Moreover, He still brings families together through hard times. He still gives us babies, and sometimes more babies than what we even asked for! God still answers prayer. He still moves mountains out of the way for those that call on Him and love Him. He enjoys a good love story, and good laugh, right alongside of a good worship service.

Do you need a miracle? Are you waiting for an answer from God? Keep listening, because He will answer. I know it. I have been there. I have waited, thinking it would never come. Then I woke up one morning and there was my answer. I would go to the doctor, and the answer would be in a report he or she held in their hands. Keep holding on, because you will be heard. Hold out for your miracle.

During one of the roughest times of my life, my brother Danny said something to me that I constantly tell other people when they are going through a tough time. He said, "Julie, God loves you. He has something so good planned for you that He is just sitting on the edge of His seat waiting. He is waiting to see the smile on your face and the dawning show in your eyes when He presents you with His gifts. He has been waiting for the right time to give to you. He cannot wait to give you something good. Just trust Him. Trust that when the time is right, He will give you that gift and then sit back and smile at the satisfaction of knowing that He once again brought a smile to your face."

As I conclude this book, as my gift to Him, I am filled with a smile. It was my promise that I would tell as many people as I possibly could of what He has done for me. However, I realize something else. I realize that this is also His gift to me!

It is forever a reminder to my family and me of the things He has done for us. The places He has brought us, and the tough times He has brought us through. So as I end, I can imagine God with a smile on His face, sitting back on His throne with His arms crossed, happy to have finally given me a gift He's been waiting to give me. The gift to Get Up and Walk: walk away from my keyboard knowing that I have done what I set out to do, because He called me to do it, and enabled me to do it. He found a way for me to tell you what He has done for my family, and what He can do for you! Time and time again, He will help you and me. Get Up and Walk…He's calling *your* name.

I love God because he listened to me, listened as I begged for mercy.

He listened intently as I laid out my case before him.
Death stared me in the face; hell was hard on my heels.
Up against it, I didn't know which way to turn;
   then I called out to GOD for help:
"Please, GOD!" I cried out. "Save my life!"
GOD is gracious—it is he who makes things right,
   our most compassionate God.
GOD takes the side of the helpless;
   when I was at the end of my rope, he saved me.
I said to myself, "Relax and rest. GOD has showered you
   with blessings.
Soul, you've been rescued from death;

Eye, you've been rescued from tears;
And you, foot, were kept from stumbling."

I'm striding in the presence of GOD,
alive in the land of the living!
I stayed faithful, though bedeviled, and despite a ton of bad luck,
Despite giving up on the human race, saying, "They're all liars
  and cheats."
What can I give back to GOD for the blessings he's poured out
  on me?
I'll lift high the cup of salvation—a toast to God!
I'll pray in the name of GOD;
I'll complete what I promised GOD I'd do,
  and I'll do it together with his people.
When they arrive at the gates of death,
GOD welcomes those who love him.
Oh, GOD, here I am, your servant, your faithful servant: set me
free for your service!
I'm ready to offer the thanksgiving sacrifice and pray in the name
  of GOD.
I'll complete what I promised GOD I'd do,
  and I'll do it in company with his people,
In the place of worship, in GOD's house…Hallelujah!

—Psalm 116 (The Message)

Acknowledgments

There is absolutely no way I could publish this book without thanking a few people who have helped me along the way. First, to my nephew Erik Staiger, for the original edits of the book, giving me encouragement and advice and for believing in the project. Your support truly means a lot. Thanks for helping me make it the BEST book possible, so we can "Kick some butt for Jesus!" My sister Diana also, for her editing advice and encouragement. I always said, "You're my sister, you're smart!" However, this takes the cake! I Love You Sis!

Andrea Hall, from Ellechor Publishing who not only took care of the final edits of the book, but also birthed the idea of "Faith Walk." Thank you Andrea for your encouragement, support, advice and for the idea of the Faith Walk. You helped me take that last step of making the book the best it could possibly be.

My Brothers and Sisters- In-Law! We are such a crazy group of people, but we love each other anyway. I do not know what I would have done without my 'smart sister' and brothers to keep me in line. Although we have our differences at times, we always rally to each other's side when it comes right down to it. I love you people!

Lynn and Jeff Minner; (they are the ones you will read about that provided our family with the ability to live in a home of our own when we became homeless, and provided us with necessities and indulgences many times throughout the years.) You both have done so much for us, without ever asking for anything in return. Lynn has also read this book for me and helped by giving advice and encouragement!

Sarah Koch; you not only read through the book to give your thoughts and advice; you have been a true friend to me. A friendship will continue for a lifetime wherever life takes either of us. I love you Sarah!

Brenda Trumbull; my partner in crime with the youth group! You are one of the best friends a girl could have, and a great ministry partner with this bunch of kids we call a youth group. Thank you for your friendship; help in ministry and for loving my family and me so much. You are always looking out for us and I appreciate it more than you know.

Wade and Jill Hall, 'Grama' Ruth, Dennis Walsh, Ethridge and Ramona Barnes, Bolivar Wesleyan Church Family, and my Grand Rapids Church Family; Thank you specifically for loving us when we have felt unloved. Thank you for taking us in when we felt lost. Thank you for helping us, when we needed to be helped. Thank you for always listening to God's direction and being a group of peoples that are committed to being Christ to one another.

Missi Watts and Carole Sarkan; thank you for your editing and personal encouragement through the beginnings of writing my story.

William "Monty" Montgomery for lighting a fire under me to write a book in the first place; Thank You!

Rochelle Carter, CEO of Ellechor Publishing; Thank you for giving me a chance to tell my story. It was a total "God Thing," that we found each other and the way that you came to have my book in your hands. Thank you for listening to Him, and for believing in me.

Last but certainly not least; to my Youth Group, thank you

guys for keeping me young! You asked if I would mention you, so here it goes—The Grand Rapids Wesleyan Youth Group is one of the greatest groups of teenagers I have ever had the privilege of knowing! As much as I love you, Jesus loves you even more! Put your trust in Him! I will always be here for ALL of you, no matter where life takes any of us. You have and will always be very special to me. We have been through so much together that no one else could ever understand. No one, that is, except Jesus. He knows, He cares, and He loves YOU!

—Love, Forever and Always, your JC (Jesus Creeper)